THE

BOOK

OF

SHED

.

THE
BOOK
OF
SHED

DESIGNING, BUILDING
AND
LOVING YOUR SHED

JOEL BIRD

Published by 535
An imprint of Blink Publishing

3.08, The Plaza,
535 Kings Road,
Chelsea Harbour,
London, SW10 0SZ

www.blinkpublishing.co.uk

facebook.com/blinkpublishing
twitter.com/blinkpublishing

Hardback – 978-1-911-274-80-3
Ebook – 978-1-911-274-81-0

A CIP catalogue of this book is available from the British Library.

Designed by Leard.co.uk
Printed and bound by Stige Arti Grafiche

3 5 7 9 10 8 6 4 2

Pictures all © the author, except for: p.16 Getty/Culture Club, p. 18 © Chronicle/ Alamy Stock Photo, p.48 Jonathan Yadin/Alamy Stock Photo, p.49 Keystone Pictures USA/Alamy Stock Photo, p.50 Getty Imagno/Contributor, p.51 Keystone Pictures USA/ Alamy Stock Photo, p.52 Getty Epics / Contributor, p.53 Trinity Mirror/Alamy Stock Photo, p.54 Getty/Ian Cook, p.55 Getty Bettmann / Contributor, p.56 Getty Arterra/ Contributor, p.93 Gerry Walden/Alamy Stock Photo, p.106 David Humphreys/ Alamy Stock Photo, p.108 Getty

Every reasonable effort has been made to trace copyright holders of material reproduced in this book, but if any have been inadvertently overlooked the publishers would be glad to hear from them.

Blink Publishing is an imprint of the Bonnier Publishing Group
www.bonnierpublishing.co.uk

'If man does not keep pace with his companions perhaps it is because he hears a different drummer. Let him step to the music he hears, however measured or far away.'

HENRY DAVID THOREAU

CONTENTS

Introduction: The Humble Shed is Changing   **9**

Part 1: Shed Conception   **15**
What's the Meaning of Shed?   17
Make Sense of Space   23
Understand the Purpose   25
Case Study: The Allotment Roof Shed   28

Part 2: Shed Inspiration   **39**
The Garden Office and Working Spaces   41
Creative Spaces   47
The Traditional Garden Shed   57
Contemporary Sheds and Shed Style   65
Case Study: The Man Temple   70
Eco Sheds and Going Green   75
Case Study: Mini Beast Mansion   82
Relaxing Spaces and the Shed Sanctuary   91
Entertaining Space   95
Small Spaces, Big Ideas   99
Tiny Houses and Beach Huts   105
Guest Rooms   111

Part 3: Before the Build   **115**
From Ideas on Paper to Project Beginnings   117
Basic Design Principles   121
Create a Design Brief   127
Understanding Cost   131
Planning Permission and Building Control   135
Case Study: The Hackney Studio   138
Building Relationships   145
Builders Merchants and Specialist Suppliers   149
A Message to the Self-Builder   155
Advice From An Old Hand   161
Case Study: The Workshop Shed   168
The Tools   177

Part 4: The Build   **195**

Shed Position and Site Preparation   197

Foundations   203

Wall Structure and Framework   211

Case Study: The Little House Shed   216

Roof Structure   225

Case Study: The Square Window Shed   232

Cladding   239

Doors and Windows   247

Water Systems and Drainage   257

Power Supply   261

Interior Finish   265

Case Study: The Walthamstow Cabin   272

Part 5: The Finished Shed   **279**

Getting to Know Your Shed   281

Maintenance   285

Being Shed   291

Useful Terms   298

Timber Joist Span Tables   300

My Shed Bookshelf   302

Acknowledgements   **304**

THE HUMBLE SHED IS CHANGING

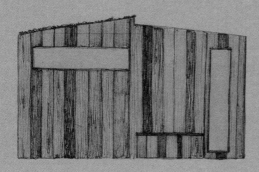
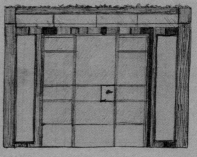

The days of small, rickety wooden structures being the sole preserve and hideaway of the middle-aged man tinkering with his model railway are at an end. The old shed, the graveyard of unused electrical appliances and unwanted furniture, is being transformed into something much more wonderful. The new 'sheddies' are dreamers, creatives and entrepreneurs. They are men and women, young and old. And while there will always be a place for the man cave, the new generation of sheds is changing the way we live and work. Sheds are opening up a world of possibilities for the most unique and underused space in our homes. This book concerns itself with this new vision of the shed. It will provide you with all the information you need to plan and create your new space by combining imaginative ideas and beautiful design with practical thinking and building knowledge.

My name is Joel Bird, in 2014 I won Channel 4's *Amazing Spaces Shed of the Year* with my allotment roof shed and I returned as a judge the year after. My day job is to design and build bespoke sheds to fit garden spaces and just as importantly to fit people's lives. In my work, I use many different sources of inspiration; I will often trawl through architectural books and research materials online. My aim is to save you time and hassle by putting all this information under one roof and at the same time pass on the knowledge I have learned over many years of shed building. By the end of the book, you will be ready to embark on your journey to create your dream space and be a part of this new shed revolution.

The book is split into sections which will guide you through your project from concept to completion.

SHED CONCEPTION will challenge you to ask yourself the right questions, to help you discover what it is you 'think' you want, and what in reality will make your life better. It will take you through basic design principles, and help you organise your thoughts and ideas into a successful design brief.

SHED INSPIRATION will illustrate the many possibilities of sheds and show you imaginative solutions to common problems. You can pick and choose the elements that are best suited for your design.

BEFORE THE BUILD and THE BUILD are practical guides, they will help you understand the building process as well as give you knowledge about tools and materials. You will learn how to predict costs and time schedules, and gain the confidence to discuss your plans with your architect or builder.

THE FINISHED SHED discusses the art of being at one with your shed.

Throughout the book there are interesting case studies of some of my own designs and builds, which take you step-by-step through the processes involved and explore the relationship my clients have with their sheds.

These projects will enable you to visualise your own build and show how you can avoid making the common mistakes that cost both time and money.

I absolutely love my job, perhaps what I love most of all is that this often small, insignificant area of the garden can have life-changing potential and I want to pass on some of this love to the readers of this book. My clients have ranged from carpenters to conceptual artists, brokers to ecologists, music producers to ordinary families, but the one thing that unites all the builds I have been involved in is the importance of creating a new, individual space.

The shed can offer an opportunity separate from where we live to... well, to do anything really – throw pots, write books, learn to dance salsa or design sheds! All of this without having to rent an office in some dreary block that you have to travel to every day. Instead, just a few steps down the garden path you can be in a whole new world, in a place that can be unique and personal to you; a place in which you can indulge your design fantasies in ways that you never can in your own house.

I live in London, where the population is larger than it has ever been at more than 8 million, and is rising by 100,000 every year. All these people need somewhere to live and work, but building brand new houses and workspace isn't the only answer; part of the solution is adapting the space we already have. Loft conversions or extensions can be very expensive and are not always possible. Often it is garden space which provides not only the most cost-effective, but also the most engaging solution to the pressures of city living.

Our needs are changing, and so too are the places in which we live. We are working from home a lot more and, since childcare is so expensive, we are often looking after our children at home too, so our lives are less rigid than the traditional 9 to 5. The shed is no longer just a place to retreat to or escape a city job, it is a way to change the way in which we live and work. The shed can bring a new freedom – a change in lifestyle, a change in job, perhaps even a chance to become self-reliant. This change in attitude to work and life and how it can be embodied in a small garden space is the revolution I am talking about, and these unusual bespoke one-offs that I build are now becoming part of the mainstream.

So, what of the future? Our cities, once synonymous with noise, dirt and cramped spaces, are trying to become better places to live in. In the UK 80% of the population are city dwellers and our urban centres must continue to absorb hundreds of thousands of people every year. This increase in population adds pressure on resources. The well-planned, super-sustainable, large-scale housing project that promotes ecological living is undoubtedly important, but I regard the new tendency towards small-scale builds, such as sheds, to also be part of the solution.

We all have our own ideas about what makes a good life and what defines progress, but the most common dilemmas I hear are from people wanting to feel like they belong to a place and a community, while at the same time being free of it and being able to express themselves on an individual level. More and more I am being asked to design a build not just for the aesthetics, but for the role it will take in redefining the client's life, and more and more I find the solution is about making our lives simpler. By simpler I mean working less, expressing ourselves more and finding peace and enjoyment in reconnecting to nature and to our communities.

So, here's to the makers of amazing sheds – the small-scale builders who like to experiment and who are in tune with their environment. They are the designers of tomorrow's urban landscape and the sheds of the next generation.

PART 1

SHED CONCEPTION

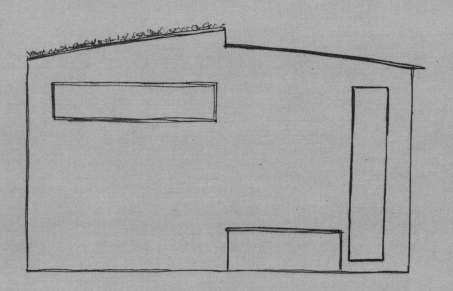

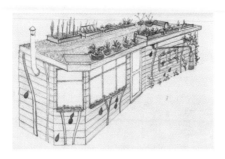

'I went to the woods because I wished to live deliberately, to front only the essential facts of life, and see if I could not learn what it had to teach, and not, when I came to die, discover that I had not lived.'

Henry David Thoreau

WHAT'S THE MEANING OF SHED?

I am often asked how I would define a shed, and over the years this question has become more and more difficult to answer. Lately, I've heard people say, 'that is not a shed!', 'a shed needs to be wooden!', 'it is too big for a shed', 'a shed should be separate from the house' and so on. It is certainly true that today's shed culture has left some people feeling a little confused. The modern shed seems to have so many names: the summer house, the garden room, the workshop, the art studio, the outhouse, the lean-to, the mid-life crisis zone. Some would argue that the shed has lost its way, but no so for me – there is an essence to the shed which remains and to understand this it is worth knowing a little about the shed's past to realise its significance in the present.

My dictionary describes the shed as 'a single-storeyed building for shelter, storage etc. especially with one or more sides open'. In fact, the definition changes with each dictionary I look in. I suppose this is a phenomenon that exists when the essence of something cannot be fully understood with a definition. The origins of the word 'shed' seem to be rooted in agricultural England, from an Old English word variously spelled 'shadde', 'shad' or 'shedde' – a dialectal variant of a specialised use of shade. The various words for shed derive from an Old Teutonic/Anglo Saxon root word for separation or division, and relate to the other meaning of shed, as in 'to shed its leaves'. The first known instance of this derivation appeared in 1481: 'A yearde in whiche was a shadde where in were six grete dogges'.

It is interesting that this first recorded version seems to describe a shed within a yard in which six, large dogs are kept, but the first written word is, of course, not the origin of the shed and does not tell the story of our human relationship to it. The origin of the shed conceptually does have roots in the keeping of animals, but earlier than that it probably began life as a storage solution. It can be argued that a shed for storage has prehistoric roots, early humans would make shelters from whatever materials could be found geographically – they built shelters from mammoth tusks and skins, for example. Whatever material was used for a primary dwelling place would also be used to make smaller storage shelters either within, outside or separate from the main space.

In time, these storage shelters probably became more specialist or used for specific purposes. In southern Italy, an archaeological study uncovered a collection of bronze tablets dating from 330–280 BC. One tablet shows inscribed in Greek exact instructions of what should be built on the land, including a shed to store straw 'measuring not less than 18 feet in length and 15 feet in width'. Another significant find in Italy of an ancient Roman settlement uncovered what can be understood as a storage section of a workshop. Excavators found a tiled roof had collapsed on top of different types of wood: olive, willow, poplar and maple. Maple wood in Roman times was used exclusively for fine furniture making which indicates the storage shed was part of a workshop that produced furniture. There is also a widespread history of the shed existing as a place to enjoy or entertain in, including the shed built as something of a folly for the wealthy. For example, the tradition of creating gardens and garden buildings for Chinese emperors and imperial families goes right back to the Shang

Dynasty (1600–1046 BC). These gardens were filled with an assortment of structures, halls and pavilions that people would move between, viewing carefully composed miniature landscapes that expressed the need for harmony between man and nature. This tradition continues through all the great Chinese dynasties.

Romans were also keen on making shelters for enjoying gardens, a version, perhaps, of our present-day 'summer houses'. The emperor Hadrian's villa at Trivoli had around sixty garden buildings. The first Roman gardens were influenced by Egyptian, Persian and Greek gardens and it was common to connect the home with the outdoors using porticos – these are perhaps akin to modern extensions, although I like to think of them as an early shed relative. European pleasure gardens originated from Greek farm gardens, and conservatories and hothouses were used to preserve foreign plants and to produce flowers and fruit out of season.

These agricultural links to the shed run right through history because they are a practical necessity, but the use of small structures as entertainment has a similar endurance. Thousands of years later wealthy follies would continue in a kind of neo-classical pastiche as seventeenth-century English aristocrats who had returned from grand tours of the continent would recreate ancient monuments. Follies were often named after the person who designed or commissioned the project. The term originates from the French word '*folie*' generally meaning madness or silliness. However, the older meaning of the word is 'delight' or 'favourite abode'. Seen by some as extravagantly useless projects, I prefer to think of them as an exercise in early British eccentricity, and the folly remains an important part of shed culture to this day.

Today, our lives are very different from those of our ancestors, but many of the principles of life remain the same. Present-day sheds vary dramatically, whether it is the traditional image we are mostly accustomed to of a modest wooden retreat, weathered and well used with old hand tools and spider web walls, or a sleek cedar summer house with underfloor heating, Wi-Fi connection and comfortable sofas, they are still manifestations of the same idea. Although separated in time by hundreds, even thousands, of years from our ancestors' early shelters and monuments, a modern shed is still a solution to the original drive to experience an alternative mindset by creating a place that is different from our primary living space.

Certainly, this need shows no signs of abating. In a recent AMA Research market report, growth for Domestic Garden Buildings and Structures for

2015 in the UK was estimated to be around 3.5%, with the total expenditure on these buildings likely to be over £325 million by 2020. The sector is influenced by a range of factors and a diversity of products, the largest segment at 35% being storage sheds, followed by an increasing demand for what are considered

to be garden buildings built for leisure activities comprising over 20% of the market. Homeworking, home improvements and a recovery in disposable income levels are suggested as being primary influences on the market. However, since growth is prevalent in all sectors of the domestic garden buildings and structures market, from lower-value sheds and greenhouses to high-value garden rooms and tree houses, I think this trend also says something about the way people are re-evaluating how they want to spend their time and money, and what they consider to be of value in their life.

The American philosopher Henry Thoreau's part memoir, part spiritual quest, *Walden*, was first published in 1854 and in it he details the experience of living for two years, two months and two days in a cabin called Walden near Massachusetts. He uses the passing seasons to symbolise human development and explores how an understanding of society can be gained through personal introspection. Thoreau meditates on the pleasures of escaping society, and reflects on the benefits of being closer to nature where time feels more as if it is ours and in doing so, I think he captures something of the 'spirit' of the shed.

'If a man does not keep pace with his companion, perhaps it is because he hears a different drummer. Let him step to the music which he hears, however measured or far away.'

My own experience is that my shed addresses a need in me which I believe is intrinsic, it is a sanctuary; a place in which I am able, if the need arises, to sit quietly and be closer to a time that existed before modern life and closer to myself. I use my shed as a kind of meditation, I try to feel the breeze as I approach, I listen to the trickle of water as it works its way off my planted roof and drips its way through guttering, watering my alpines and succulents on its journey to the floor. I can smell the dusty books and pine resin as I sit down at my desk with a cup of tea and prepare to write or paint, and I immediately feel more connected to the world around me and this connection seems to reset my mind and makes me feel happier.

This is my personal shed relationship – yours will be unique to you because the meaning of shed is whatever gives your shed meaning. Yes, your shed can be extra storage for your cluttered life, but it doesn't have to be just one thing, because there are no rules. This versatility is part of the shed's appeal and the reason its spirit has survived and will continue to survive. The shed's magnificence is in the infinite possibilities that lie in the imagination of its creator. Your shed can be a monument to the time in your life that you were happiest or it can signal the start of a new way of being. It can reflect your ideas and opinions of the world as it is, or it can be a fantasy world which only exists when you walk through your shed door. So, let your mind wander and your imagination expand, and start on a journey that will see you become at one with your shed... Welcome to *The Book of Shed*.

MAKE SENSE OF SPACE

You will have a rough idea about what your shed will be, but the more you understand about sheds the more equipped you will be to design something that is right for you. The transformation of ideas into an actual building can be quite daunting and the multitude of variables in design, structure, materials and so on can be overwhelming. If you can break up the ideas and the information into a series of smaller connected aspects, it will make your life easier and the whole process will seem more logical and more manageable.

The shed should be a personal expression of your own ideas, since we are all individuals in this world, each shed should be in its own way unique. However, it is a good idea to have some direction. Before we can express ourselves properly it is important to understand the boundaries, I am not talking about confining the imagination, but the inevitable limits that life provides. Understanding boundaries will help bring into view the problems you may need to overcome.

The boundaries for a shed build are the space in which you have to build, the rules within which you are allowed to build and the amount of money or time you have with which to build.

Your first steps are to physically understand what space you do have and at this point you should mark out where you think the shed will go in your garden, then take some rough measurements. Your shed needs to be large enough for its purpose, a shed that is too small may not provide you with everything you imagine, and a shed that is too large can overpower your garden and needlessly eat into your outside space. A beautiful, well-proportioned shed can add value to your house, one that takes over your garden can potentially devalue your house. You may be unsure at this point about the scale, shape or orientation of your build; this will become clearer as you start to understand what designs you like and what you intend the shed to be used for. If you are still unsure about these elements, then make an approximation so you have something to roughly work with.

Next, it is good to get an idea of the parameters within which you are allowed to build in your area. Each country and each area within that country will have its own set of guidelines for permitted development, building regulations and advice for getting planning permission. For example in the UK, it is often the case that a build of $15m^2$ under 2.5m in height will not need either planning permission or require the involvement of building control.

The measurements you have taken will give you a rough understanding of the cost for your build, this obviously fluctuates depending on who is doing the work and what the design of the build is, but it will give you a good idea of estimates for buying materials. What you can do is formulate an idea of what your budget is based on, what you would like to spend and what you can afford. My advice is to not underestimate your shed either in terms of money or in value. A good shed can provide the most cost-effective solution to creating space, and it will give you and your family a great deal of joy. Spending more money on your shed can be a sensible economic decision as well as a practical one.

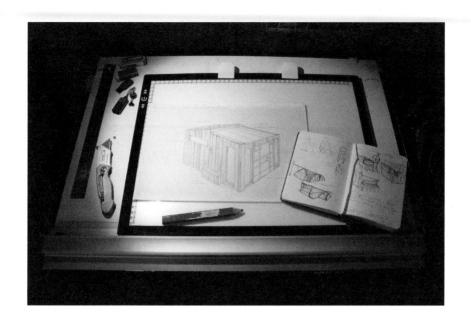

UNDERSTAND THE PURPOSE

The first question I ask my clients when designing a shed is: what will you be using your shed for? This might seem obvious, but people often get distracted by their ideas and the abundance of design possibilities and forget what the original reason for the new space was. The purpose of the shed should drive the design and not the other way around.

If your shed is a workspace, perhaps a workshop or an art studio, then the placement of the windows, the amount of shelving and size of your work bench are more important than any cosy seating areas or home comforts, and vice versa if the space is designed as a place to relax. Perhaps your intention is to design a shed that will allow you to pursue a new career or change the way you live your life, in such cases you may need to allocate part of your budget to the acquisition of tools or equipment, which may result in a simpler and cheaper exterior.

You should try to be as honest as possible with yourself, if your shed is a practical solution to having too much stuff in the house, or to house teenage family members, then you should concentrate on maximising

the area of your build rather than spending money on making it your work station. Or if the purpose of your shed is a means with which to express yourself either aesthetically or philosophically, these are just as valid reasons as being practical and it should be designed with this in mind, and you should not feel pressured into making it available for storage.

It is often the case with a family house that a shed needs to be multifunctional, so I try to challenge my clients to write down the different things that the shed will be used for and what will be necessary to make their space function properly. Then I ask them to create a hierarchy by putting these functions in order of importance. You should prioritise the most important roles your shed plays and you should allocate more space to things you will spend more time doing; this is not an exact science, but it can help you focus the mind on the real purpose of your shed.

CASE STUDY

The Allotment Roof Shed
Approximate size: 15m²

The Brief

When I had the idea of building my own shed, the design brief I gave myself was to create a supremely functional workspace. I wanted every square inch of the shed to have a purpose. There needed to be a space for working on artwork, for writing, a place to make music and the potential for a small workshop. I wanted to feel comfortable in the shed, I definitely didn't want it to be too tidy and I was also keen for the shed to have some green credentials and preferably a living roof.

The Design

My own shed was the first-ever shed I built. I wanted to use it as an experiment to understand the potential of this small space, but I also wanted the shed to change the way I lived my life. At the time of designing my shed, I had just moved back to London and I was wondering what to do with my

life. I knew I had a passion for creative work, but I also knew many people who had moved to London to be artists and musicians and because of the financial strains were forced to get better paid jobs and were never creative again; I used to call it the 'London Conundrum', a problem which exists in all big cities.

Being any kind of an artist is partly the act of creating, but just as important is the ability to design a life that makes the creative part possible. I knew I couldn't afford to rent an art studio and a music studio, so my shed fast became the incentive that would make this creative life a possibility.

Part of making this lifestyle a reality meant changing the amount of money I would spend on everyday living. I have been interested in keeping my bills lower ever since I left home, so as to give me more time to be creative. I think back with frugal fondness to my first London flat and the way I lived;

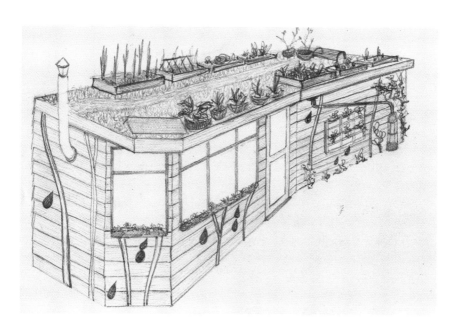

I had an electric meter in which I put pound coins to turn on the power; it was great training – I knew exactly how much energy each of my appliances gave me and I kept a record of what worked best.

For example, in the winter, from one boiled kettle, I would make a cup of tea, then I would fill a small flask so I had another cup of tea for later, then I would fill two small water bottles, one would go into my bed which would stay warm all night and the other would go inside the coat I was wearing. This meant I would seldom use a heater and my pound would go a long way. It was this type of living that allowed me to work a part-time job so I could keep painting, keep playing music and keep paying rent.

At the time of designing my shed, the other major expense in my life was buying nice food, by 'nice' I really mean fresh, this is one of the reasons I always wanted an allotment. The idea of producing a little home-grown food was something I had dreamed of almost as much as a shed. Since there was no room in my garden, I thought I would literally lift the ground space beneath the shed onto the roof. So, instead of having a shed on an allotment I would have an allotment on a shed. This was a kind of Eureka moment, one which galvanised the whole project; the design was no longer just a space – the shed had a personality of its own, and personality is important for any build.

The Build

When I decided to make a shed for my garden, the act of building wasn't new to me. After first moving to London, I worked with my cousin on loft conversions, so in this time I learned about how a build should be structurally.

My shed is on a concrete slab. I don't often pour slabs anymore, partly because of the environmental impact and also because limited access means I would have to carry all the materials and machinery through somebody's house.

I knew since it was quite a large shed and there was going to be a fair amount of weight in the garden roof I had planned, that it would be more efficient and safer to build the framework out of wood from a timber merchant. But after the basic framework was built, I was able to piece together much of the build out of recycled materials.

The windows and doors were taken out of my house when I replaced them with new ones; the majority of the cladding was recycled from old fencing and I made some myself by ripping down logs from the local parks and allotments. The soil for the garden roof was taken from the hole I dug for the slab and I also made use of internet auctions and recycle sites for materials such as the flooring; you often get people selling or giving away miscalculated orders that you can use on these small-scale builds.

The roof consisted of 18mm Water and Boil Proof (WBP) plywood sitting on the framework which was then sealed with torch-on bitumen roofing felt. This was also the first time I had made a living roof; I knew the basics of what plants needed to grow – water, light and drainage – and sometimes a basic knowledge can be enough, especially since nature will often power on regardless. I protected the roof with a roll of old synthetic fabric I had bought from a charity shop, used gravel for drainage and then a mix of sharp sand and soil as the substrate.

The interior was also clad using recycled wood, but I did purchase some materials for the studio because I wanted to make it as soundproof as possible, albeit on a tight budget. I began by filling the space between the upright joists with acoustic Rockwool insulation and then fitted acoustic sound board, which is dense plasterboard. Density is sometimes a neglected part of soundproofing, but it is especially important for the bass frequencies. I then added a layer of thick carpet, which I got free from a neighbour, and another layer of sound board – the idea of this was to create a cheap form of decoupling (this interrupts the sound wavelengths and therefore weakens the overall noise that can penetrate through. Finally, came a layer of fabric I again bought from a charity shop, which just makes it look nicer and acts as a further sound dampener.

I had a budget of £2,000 – although this is unrealistic for large-scale builds, the fact that I avoided labour costs by building it myself and that much of the materials used were recycled meant I managed to build the shed for around £1,000. The shell was built in a couple of weeks and the build was basically finished in around a month, but since 'completion' I have continued to work on my shed, adding things and taking things away. I think good sheds change with you – they evolve and become what you want them to be over time.

The Finished Shed

Now that my shed is built and I have been using it for a few years, I have a good idea about the realities of using the space and what has worked best for me. My shed is not a place I perceive as escaping to as I thought it might be; I see it as a place I go to exist, but this is partly due to the lifestyle change which the shed has helped bring about. As we spend more time doing things we like to do and want to do, the less we see these things as an escape and more as a way of life.

The front section, which is roughly 4m x 2m, is where I paint, sculpt and where I design other people's sheds; it is also where I am now sitting writing this book. I managed to squeeze in a small desk area which is just 900mm wide and 600mm deep – it is a simple set-up, but the simplicity helps me concentrate. This area is more about the change of headspace than anything else, I have books around me for reference and I always try to have plants around me when I am being creative – it makes my work better.

I used as many windows in this section as I could. I store my frames – which go on to be used to stretch my canvases – around the windows, so the light continues to enter the shed and this has also become part of the shed's look and personality. In hindsight, I think I might have considered putting in a small roof window as well.

I have a large foldaway bench on which I paint and sculpt while standing up because I find stand-up benches are better for me physically when working for long periods. Although the benches fold away, in truth they are nearly always in use. Indeed, one of the reasons I wanted a specific place to paint away from the house is so that the paintings can be left out to be worked on. I like to let my work 'brew' in my mind, so it helps to be able to see the work and alter it in the given moment that inspiration is present. It can also be difficult making the transition between the functional tasks of daily life and the mindset needed to be creative; it is important to avoid any more psychological barriers than are necessary, and the act of having to find and set up materials for a project can be enough to discourage any tired artist.

This front section is also a nice place to just sit and have a cup of tea to take away the stresses of life. I have a small wood burner and an old Arabian camel seat to sit on. This little corner of the shed is the closest thing I have to a little retreat. I will often make a brew, usually a green tea from leaves, and this short ritual is enough to reset my thoughts.

The heat a wood burner pumps out can be quite substantial, so I bought the smallest one I could find and it is more than enough to heat the space. I only use it in the winter time and I always leave the door of the wood burner open when not in use because once a great tit flew down the flue pipe and got trapped, but luckily I heard it flapping around and released it.

The music studio is entered through an old wooden interior door – again this came from my house when I was renovating. The studio is roughly 3m x 3m running at an angle and was designed this way so as to have less impact on my garden space. I use it for recording, mixing and as a live practice room, so the area had to be reasonably square for practical reasons. Generally speaking, a longer space with a higher roof would have better acoustic properties for mixing, but it was a case of compromising to fit all intended uses. I have also learned since recording in my studio that the room would have benefitted from a little more 'life': by which I mean a little sound reflection, so I would have probably used less material for sound dampening and used specific acoustic panels such as bass traps in the corners, but this is easy to rectify should I wish to.

It was important for me to get a drum kit into the room. I have a tama jazz kit with a smaller kick drum which takes up less room. I purposely planned the drum kit to squeeze into the smaller angled corner of the room, the other right-angled corners house my Rhodes piano and my computer and mixing area. Along the right-hand side is a wall of stringed instruments kept out of the way on some guitar hangers that I bought cheap from a local music studio, which was throwing them out.

Now to the outside, at the rear of the shed I have a bike repair station and tool storage; this is covered by a small, tiled overhang on which sits my tin bath. I use this space more like a traditional shed, it was important for me to have an area to just mess about in, to take things apart, to repair things and if I am using any solvent-based products it is good to have an outside area to avoid breathing fumes.

Around the front of the shed I have built a little staircase which leads through my elder tree onto the allotment roof. I grow a whole variety of fruit and vegetables up here. I am no expert on gardening, but over the years I have learned enough to get some decent crops and this learning is all part of the fun. Each year I try a few new types of crop, the most successful of which I will grow again. This year I focused on leaks, carrots, potatoes, strawberries, rhubarb and tomatoes. Originally I wanted to be able to grow the vegetables to make my own Scouse stew, but these days I prefer to grow things that taste better than produce from supermarkets.

I spend long periods of time on my allotment roof. I pick whatever crops are ready for harvesting, I relax on a little bench at the back or I even have a soak with a book in my tin bath. I also have a small stove up there and will often warm up some vegetables and make a little toasted sandwich. Over the back of my shed are the local public allotments and it really is like a mini countryside as I peer over at the other allotmenteers hard at work.

I especially love to sit up on the roof when I come back from a shed-building work day. Often the London commute has been a long one. Sitting quietly in nature seems to help my constitution, partly because of its beauty, but also because of the inspiration it offers me. Nature has a tremendous work ethic, and I try to reproduce its relentless incremental growth in my own work. I think it was Matisse who had an allotment, and every morning he would go and sit with the artichokes; he would use them as a kind of meditation to feed his creativity. My shed reminds me that I am a part of nature and that the act of working makes us who we are.

I find in my work as a shed designer that there has been a shift towards sustainability, partly for ethical reasons and partly because it makes practical and economic sense. The eco credentials of my shed are more significant than you might think. The wood burner and solar-powered lighting help keep the bills to a minimum, I am also cutting out the daily commute to a studio. Plus, although the crops I grow are never going to replace the weekly shop, they do help, especially in the summer months, and if I can get a couple of meals a week out of my produce, by the end of the year this makes quite a difference. But I have to say, what is most rewarding is the feeling you get from being more self-reliant; it is just so good to be working and producing in my shed, knowing that I am completely sustainable while doing so.

It is also perhaps worth considering what the word 'eco' means to you. For me it is about having an ethical outlook to the environment; sustainability is important for this, but for my shed to have a true eco ethos I wanted to involve and support some wildlife. I cultivate wildflowers on the roof for bees and butterflies, and I try to let some of my crops flower and go to seed for this reason. I also don't keep my shed, or my garden for that matter, too clean and tidy as a bit of mess encourages beetles and spiders – all of which aids biodiversity.

Conclusion

I think ultimately the best thing about my shed is that it makes my life better. I spend more time in (or on) my shed, than I do in my house, it has taught me that I do not necessarily need all the things I own and I can honestly say I am a happier person since I built the shed. I genuinely believe anyone can do this; for a relatively small investment of time and money, a shed can make a huge impact on your life. My shed has allowed me to work, live more sustainably, it is the place where I feel most at home, where I work and create the things that make me who I am and, more than any other object or space, it's the shed that defines me.

PART 2

SHED INSPIRATION

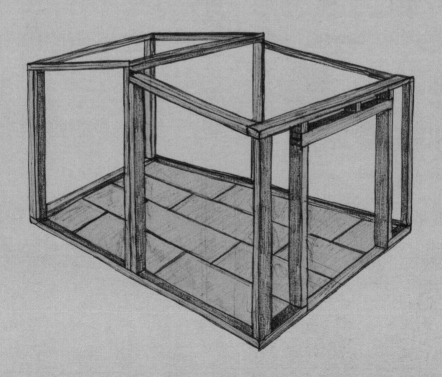

'The vocation, whether it be that of the farmer or the architect, is a function; the exercise of this function as regards the man himself is the most indispensable means of spiritual development, and as regards his relation to society the measure of his worth.'

Ananda K. Coomaraswamy

THE GARDEN OFFICE AND WORKING SPACES

Our work defines us. In the past it has determined where we spend our time, who we spend that time with and what we spend our time doing. The shed as a workplace is changing how we live and work, and of the shed uses it is the 'working shed' that has seen the most dramatic growth. The shed workplace has many advantages. There is no spirit-crushing commute; within a few steps you can be at work. You can choose your work hours; if you are an early riser you can get started before the sun rises and finish your day at lunch time or, if like me you prefer to ease into the day, you can get into your stride just as everybody else is driving home. It is also a much more beautiful place to work; with a shed you can combat work fatigue by glancing out of the window to see garden birds feeding or watch trees sway in the breeze.

The single greatest factor in making the shed office possible is our recent dramatic advances in technology and the improvements in affordability and accessibility of this technology. The arrival of a world in which we can walk to the end of our garden and have a global connection at our fingertips has transformed the way we work.

This idea of the new connected shed is far-reaching, from financial services to consultancy, from journalism to publishing. Most creative people I know who are managing to make a living in industries such as design, animation, film editing and music production have all benefitted, if not completely transformed their lives, with this new way of working.

Any avoidance of the draining commute is definitely a good thing, but this ease of journey to the shed does of course go both ways, and the trip back to the living room for a sneaky sandwich and nap becomes a possibility that was previously a difficult feat to pull off. Undoubtedly self-discipline comes into play here, but this is aided by creating a work environment that you feel comfortable in; if you physically want to be in your workplace, you are much more likely to get some work done. It is also good to make your work shed as self-contained as possible, if for you too there is a direct correlation between the caffeine levels in your blood and your ability to work, then it can be a good idea to make an area with a kettle to avoid breaking the sacrosanct rule and going back to the house.

Working from home is probably the dream for many people, but you have to take it seriously if you're going to pay the bills. Taking your work seriously means getting exactly what you need in your shed to allow you to work well. If you need an expensive ergonomic chair or an A3 scanner or a new potter's wheel, then you need to budget for this early on. If the shed is designed as a workplace, the tools within it are just as important as the space itself.

It really depends on the type of work you are doing as to how you set up your shed. Storage is essential to most working environments and it is important to consider the size and position of things such as shelving at the same time as the more obvious equipment such as your desk. Tidy wiring will also benefit you, I am seldom less happy than when I am stuffed down the back of a desk untangling strangled wires in near darkness. If you need to be unplugging devices often then make them accessible by putting the sockets above the desk instead of below.

Order means efficiency, but you also don't want to make your workplace a boring and sterile environment. It is perhaps intuitive to recreate the generic workspaces that you are used to, but this is your chance to create the place you want to work in. Think about what makes a place comfortable for you, it may involve natural light, temperature or peace and quiet; then think about what you need to work efficiently, this may be tidiness, open space or quality tools – by combining the two you are going to have an environment in which you are happy working.

Consider who will use the shed and what it will predominantly be used for. The fewer distractions you have from working the better, so keep the space as directly associated with work as you possibly can. This is not always possible with a busy family life, but you should at least try to get some rules in place, such as for certain hours it will be used solely as a workspace. If your shed is going to be used for meetings, consider how you would like your clients to experience the shed. My shed acts as a kind of showroom at times, for this I don't need to change much, so if your business is creative it is ok to let your imagination be on show, but if your business is about being organised, perhaps you want to think about a tidy space to give the right impression.

Don't forget about security, again technology has improved this area lately, there are now cameras and alarm systems available at very affordable prices. And it is still worth using the old methods of a good strong padlock to stop thieves. Even if they manage to get in through a window, it can be just as useful to stop them getting out of the door with your possessions.

Since the shed has the potential to transform the way in which we work, it is also worth thinking about your relationship to work and the type of work you would like to do if given the opportunity.

Your shed can act as a statement of intent or even perhaps the catalyst to a change in job. Remember that the current scenario of how and where we work is not something that has always been so. For the centuries preceding the industrial revolution, cottage industries were the predominant form of work thus the connection between home and work was much stronger.

We rightly perceive our lives as fortunate when comparing them to the incredible hardships and suffering of the working classes during the industrial revolution, but the working existence that we are used to is still largely influenced by this period.

In the modern age, individuals are asking themselves what they want from their working life, and re-evaluating what is important. We are seeing a surge in careers that involve multiple part-time jobs, often including creative freelance work, or individuals switching to flexible working to start businesses of their own.

When it comes to shed work and the multi-career option, I am no exception to the rule. I would say I have designed a lifestyle whereby I am working as an artist, musician, shed designer and a writer. Each job helps to support the other and the fluctuations in work patterns are compensated by each job meaning there is no real downtime. I am also happier for it, my work life is something I look forward to and the change in work means I seldom get tired of anything I do.

The places of work, the hours we work and the types of work we do are questions not just for the individual but for society. By supporting flexible work hours and a workspace at home, we are learning that there is an economic benefit to shed work as well as an ethical one. Indeed, this captures the whole essence of designing your own workspace. The working shed has the potential to allow the individual to exist within a company and within society while having a sense of purpose. Our work, after all, should be something that gives both society and us worth.

'Imagination is the beginning of creation. You imagine what you desire; you will what you imagine, and at last you create what you will.'

George Bernard Shaw

CREATIVE SPACES

The creative shed has an undoubted magic, it is a place that resonates with a different headspace. A refuge from society, from conformism, it reconnects the artist with nature and disconnects us from the domestication which dampens the creative will. Its use as a place to bring into existence great works of cultural significance should not be underestimated. The shed has produced not just good work, but great and important artistic pieces from an expanse of working fields. The list of people who give credence to this is substantial, from writers such as Mark Twain, Charles Dickens, Virginia Woolf and Dylan Thomas, to composers such as Gustav Mahler and Edvard Greig. The creative shed provides the solitary peace and quiet needed for the long periods of concentration which set free conventional thought patterns and draw the mind ever closer to a spiritual world which is so essential to producing the masterpiece.

Indeed, masterpieces of the highest order were created in shed-like space by the celebrated composer Gustav Mahler in the later part of the nineteenth century. Mahler had an aversion to noise, and his need for a place away from people led him to commission the building of a composer's hut close to where he and his family stayed during the summer, in the tiny town of Steinbach, within the spectacular lake and mountain region of Salzkammergut outside of Salzburg, Austria. He eventually had three composing huts built, one in Toblach which is now Dobbiaco, in Italy (*below*), and one in Maiernigg, nestled in the secluded woods on the shore of the Worthersee.

Inside his shed stood a desk and a Baby Grand Piano, the only music in the room other than his own was that of Bach – a composer he admired greatly. He kept the manuscripts locked in a wall safe, and his bookshelf contained all the works of Goethe and of the philosopher Kant. It was at this first shed in Steinbach he composed his third Nature Symphony, a celebration of the natural world in all its forms. Nature was a huge source of inspiration for Mahler and the composer's huts provided in his words, 'peace, security and Dionysiac wonder.'

Most of us do not have access to such majestic wonder and, when glancing out of our shed windows, are unlikely to see lakes bordered by steep mountain pinnacles reflecting from the shores of the Attersee, but the principles of making a separate space in which we can exist on a more creative level do translate. We can after all only make the most out of the environment we do have, but what we do have is often more than we might realise.

Whether you are designing, building or adapting your shed, think about what you are going to need in order to create, both practically and spiritually. It is important that you have the physical space and the right tools for the job at hand, and by tools I don't just mean tenon saws and sets of chisels. Tools can be anything from a lathe to a laptop. Some of us will need technology to create, others will want to keep their shed technology-free to avoid distractions.

It is equally important to feel comfortable in your creative environment. By feeling relaxed in your shed it is going to be much easier to harness inspiration and bring ideas to the front of your mind. Consider the external world and ask yourself questions in relation to it. For example, if you are susceptible to the cold it is going to be important to get the right insulation and heating into your creative shed because if you feel cold, the mind is going to be taken up with the feeling of stress instead of being filled with ideas.

Consider what type of lighting you will need, up-lighting will help to avoid shadows and task lighting on work benches will help with detailed work such as painting, embroidery or cabinet making. If you need to get an accurate understanding of colours, then natural light is essential and likewise if you need to isolate a computer screen then an ability to block out light is important. If sunlight is especially useful to you then map the path of the sun and use large windows or even a skylight to drag in the maximum amount of light, or if you work in the summer months or in a hot climate then the creation of shade will be of more importance.

The Irish playwright George Bernard Shaw (*above*) had a clever solution to the problems of enticing light into his tiny shed. Situated in the small village of Ayot St Lawrence in Hertfordshire, he worked for the last 20 years of his life in what can be considered relative sophistication for the times. In addition to the shed having electricity, a telephone and a buzzer system, it would rotate to follow the sun using a revolving mechanism. Shaw appropriated the shed from his wife and, at the time, revolving sheds of this type were actually mass-manufactured in Northern Europe for use at tuberculosis sanatoriums.

The revolving building is making somewhat of a comeback in architectural circles because of the very benefits that attracted Bernard Shaw to it. By turning the shed towards the light, you can potentially keep windows to a minimum since large expanses of glass are usually used to maximise the light as the sun moves along its path throughout the day, and the fewer windows a building has, the easier it is to heat in cold weather. If you are working in direct sunlight in the summer months, a revolving build also means you can turn away from the sun towards the shade to cool down.

How you understand your work environment and adapt it to your creative processes has the potential to affect your work dramatically. External elements can make a difference internally to your creative state of mind so try to understand yourself as well as the creative work you do to make a shed that works properly.

Let us not forget that the creative fields are very much about work, 'genius is 1% inspiration 99% perspiration' to quote the great American inventor and

entrepreneur Thomas A. Edison, and I might add shed worker (*Left*, alongside Henry Ford and outside the shed where he created the first lightbulb. Edison also had his own glass-blowing shed where the bulbs were crafted for his experiments). The hard work involved in following artistic endeavour is very much understood by successful artists and when designing your creative shed there are many similarities to the work shed.

Working efficiently requires practicality. For example, if you need deliveries, perhaps for making tables, metal working or glass blowing, consider your access to get the raw materials in and out of your studio space. Think about using storage to keep your work surfaces and floor space tidy, and use a logical labelling system to keep your various tools accessible. The tools you use most should be within reach, the objects you do not use should be stored away to maximise the space you do have.

Undoubtedly a tidy workplace can be efficient, but it is not necessarily good for the imagination and sometimes the creative mind needs some chaos to loosen the familiar structures and thought patterns of conformity. One such creative sheddie was sculptor Henry Moore, who had several converted stables at his home in Perry Green, Hertfordshire, and his sheds were at the heart of his creative process. Photographs of how he left the studios on his death in 1986 show a cacophony of shaped objects strewn about the walls and floors, bits and pieces of unfinished sculptures, and of maquettes and animal bones including an enormous elephant skull.

Moore (*above*) is quite a hero of mine, the son of a coal miner, he is probably best known for his, semi-abstract carved marble and cast bronze sculptures. His ability in later life to fulfil large-scale commissions made him a very wealthy man. Despite this he lived frugally and most of the money he earned went to the Henry Moore Foundation, which supports education and promotion of the arts. It is probably not especially sensible to judge our own work by comparing it to prolific geniuses of this ilk, but it is always useful to learn about how they worked. Henry Moore seemed to fill his studio with objects that would be inspirational and useful to producing his next work, this is its own kind of practicality.

It is the responsibility of a creative person to understand what they will need to produce work. So, if you are an artist it may be important to evoke the feeling that you experience when making a work, perhaps a sense of time or place. If you are a writer, it could be that a certain environment is going to allow you to bring forth feelings of passion that you need for your work

– feelings of love or anger or wisdom. You may need to allow for a place in which you can absorb the world around you, to let your ideas and feelings about a subject brew; it might be that you decide to introduce a bed to your shed to participate in that great friend of the creative – the restorative nap.

I know some artist friends who do not want to be tainted by their previous works and reject displaying them in any form; I prefer to have things I value around me because I want to remember what it was about a piece that I liked and use it to give me some direction if I feel lost.

If you are of the latter disposition, use clipboards or magnetic pins to display pictures and ideas from your current project, or perhaps you have posters or a quote that holds the essence of what you want the body of your work to express. Have words or phrases around you, let them cross your senses and don't be afraid to let words influence your visual art or vice versa.

The Welsh poet Dylan Thomas wrote various masterpieces from his shed (*above*), including 'Over Sir John's Hill' in which he describes the views from his shed and the defiant classic that seems to capture a part of his rebellious soul 'Do Not Go Gentle Into That Good Night'. The 'bike shed study' as he called it, among other things, sits on the cliff above the boathouse in Laugharne, Carmarthenshire, where he spent the last four years of his life. Perched on stilts, the shed overlooks a spectacular view of the Taf Estuary and the Gower Peninsula below. He filled his 'word-splashed hut' with pictures of Lord Byron, Walt Whitman, Louis MacNeice, W. H. Auden and William Blake. Alongside lists of alliterative and rhyming words, he also had a painting by Modigliani, picaresque nudes and serial specials from Picture Post magazine.

Inspiration is the most elusive of all the aspects involved in the creation of artistic work. I have always enjoyed using music to help lubricate the imagination. If I am writing, certain classical pieces or peaceful hypnotic music will not collide with the space in the mind that formulates words. When painting or sculpting, I like to listen to particular albums, I quite like the structure of around 45 minutes of work time before a break so I can have 'new eyes' again ready to adjust my work. I also like to have plants around me when I work, I find it subconsciously gives my work a more complex structure and this transcends the visual arts into writing words or composing music.

People work and create in different ways, what matters in art is the concept that creativity is king. The ability to make whatever environment you need to produce your masterpiece is a skill in itself. Your shed should ultimately feel like your little creative hideaway. We all have our own quirks and unusual habits – I think of these as gifts sent from our subconscious mind to help us structure or navigate through our thoughts, so it is important to respect these and let our personality breathe a little.

Take Roald Dahl's mythical little writing shed (*right*), his 'inner sanctum' or his 'little nest' as he called it. Sitting between a lush avenue of interweaving lime trees in Great Missenden, Buckinghamshire, it was specifically made for him by a local builder in the 1950s. The idea for it came to Dahl after he had visited Dylan Thomas's shed in Wales. As Quentin Blake, Roald Dahl's celebrated illustrator remarks, 'the whole of the inside was organised as a place for writing... he didn't want to move from his chair, everything was within reach.'

He would write on an ancient wing-backed armchair which had belonged to his mother, with a piece of wood perched across the bows, the

simple writing desk would sit on a roll of corrugated paper laid across his legs, his feet would rest on an old travelling trunk full of logs nailed to the floor. He didn't like writing at a desk because he had hurt his back as an RAF pilot during a crash landing in the Second World War. When he later developed an abscess in his back, his response was not to get a new chair, but to hack a hole in the back of the one he had to accommodate the sore.

Roald Dahl (*above*) was a highly disciplined writer and ensconced himself in his hut for around four hours every day for 30 years. He would write only on yellow legal pads imported from America. Before writing, he would sharpen six of his favourite Dixon Ticonderoga pencils with an electric pencil sharpener, using an inscribed clothes brush from his boarding school days to sweep away the shavings. When the pencils had been sufficiently blunted he knew he had been writing for around two hours.

His daughter Ophelia Dahl recalled of the shed in an article for the *Daily Mail*, 'Inside, it had a very mercurial atmosphere, the sense of an inventing room or laboratory'. On the table within reach of his writing chair was a curious and macabre collection of objects including a hip bone that he kept after his hip replacement, a large ball of foil wrappers – evidence of the boiled sweets he sucked for inspiration and an ashtray filled with Marlboro stubs. On the walls, pinned with bent paperclips, were the letters and drawings from his children as well as a quote from Degas saying 'art is a lie to which one gives the accent of truth' and a photograph of his daughter Olivia who tragically died of measles encephalitis at the age of just seven.

Dahl's hut was built specifically for his art form. There are those of us who do not know exactly what it is we want to make or which direction we are travelling in creatively; nevertheless I think it is perfectly possible for the shed to enliven the creative forces within you. Sometimes you need to build a space and spend some time within it to understand what it tells you about yourself and what you should create. Maybe just the act of building your shed, of using tools or thinking about materials will help to inspire you to create something new of your own.

The great American playwright and novelist Arthur Miller (*above*) built his own shed from scratch saying, 'It was purely an instinctive act... I had never built a building in my life'. On writing *Death of a Salesman*, he had the kernel of an idea while building the shed: 'the ideas were bound up within the construction itself. I kept saying, as soon as I get the roof on and the windows in, I'm gonna start this thing'. When it was serviceable, his impulse was just 'to sit in the middle of it, and shut the door, and let things happen'; by the end of that day, he had written the first act of one of the most famous plays of the twentieth century. Personally, I think throughout the play you get a sense that the shed he built somehow changed him and became part of the work. In the words of Biff, the son of Willy (the salesman) in Act One:

'Well, I spend six or seven years after high school trying to work myself up. Shipping clerk, salesman, business of one kind or another. And it's a measly manner of existence. To get on that subway on the hot mornings in summer. To devote your whole life to keeping stock, or making phone calls, or selling or buying. To suffer fifty weeks of the year for the sake of a two week vacation, when all you really desire is to be outdoors with your shirt off.'

Ultimately, it doesn't matter what other people think or say, it is up to you to create a space in which you feel safe and secure enough to allow your imagination to roam and run free. The separateness that the shed provides makes it a magical place in which ideas and dreams are born and if you can provide the work ethic to accompany this magic then wonderful things can happen. Give your imagination the opportunity to grow and, who knows, it might just flourish.

'You are only here for a short visit.
Don't hurry. Don't worry.
And be sure to smell the
flowers along the way.'

Walter C. Hagen

THE TRADITIONAL GARDEN SHED

With all our modern extravagances and new expansive ideas of the shed, it is quite easy to forget the traditional garden shed and for many, including me, it is perhaps still the greatest shed of all. The humble garden shed has such a strong lineage to our past that it says much about us as humans. I have more than just an affection for the garden shed, I have a respect for it; it has always been a part of our lives and it probably always will be.

Our garden sheds can be traced back to early European gardens, although it can be argued agricultural links go right back to the beginnings of crop growing. The tradition of the shed used for storage runs the course of history because it is hard to improve upon its simple, practical solution to this necessity.

My respect and affection for the garden shed started with my allotment shed, which was really the first shed I spent any significant amount of time in. 'Humble' is a word I hear said about the garden shed, not least by me. I think in the case of my allotment shed, decrepit might be more accurate. But as is so often the case, our affections grow from that which has flaws and

the list of flaws that my allotment shed had might render my affections overwhelming!

It smelled of earth and car oil that had been used to try and preserve the wood, I'm guessing. A car battery sat on the shelf powering a small transistor radio, next to it was a set of stiff wooden drawers that housed half-used seed packets. There was straw on the floor and an old tin bucket to catch the leak from the corrugated tin roof. Soil had worked its way into every nook and cranny, you couldn't enter the shed for a second without both you and your clothes needing a long soak afterwards. It was dark, it was filthy, it was beautiful... I loved it.

I would sit inside with my flask of tea listening to Radio 4 as the pattering of rain hit the tin roof and a blackbird song echoed slightly in the near distance; I watched with a quiet mind as the world fed the crops I had just planted, nothing ever quite lived up to the peace I experienced in those moments. How could one ever look upon this shack with anything but affection. Although this is perhaps the shed I loved most of all, this level of decrepitude is not for everyone and it is still possible to have affection for something that works to the best of its capabilities.

The main problem with the garden shed is the junkyard phenomenon that is the fate of so many of its kind. The sad image of this little structure piled high with boxes of old photographs that have long since gone mouldy, its doorway blocked with an entanglement of outgrown children's bikes, is a scenario familiar to us all. The answer to this problem is to give the garden shed a promotion, think bigger – it will make your life easier if you provide enough space to either properly house family storage or store the junk elsewhere.

If we disregard the junkyard shed, most people consider the traditional garden shed to be potting shed related. The garden or potting shed can be both the aesthetic focal point and the utilitarian hub of a garden. It can be absolutely crucial to a functioning garden and you should therefore carefully

consider what its uses will be, where it will be placed and what will be placed around it. When designing your garden shed, you should make drawings of not just the shed but the whole garden to understand how the outside space will be used.

Think practically, it makes sense to group items together in a garden space. Consider designing a hard-surfaced working area that might contain your shed, a greenhouse, a composter and an incinerator. With potting sheds, it is especially useful to collect the rainwater from the roof into a water butt since the shed will almost certainly be used at some point to propagate plants. If you are going to use the shed as somewhere to just relax, we are entering the realms of the summer house and perhaps you do not want to sit next to the smell of a compost heap, but in true potting shed style I think the compost heap is better close by to make it work more efficiently and the smell becomes 'familiar' after a while.

Many garden designers tend to screen off sheds from the garden area if they feel it is spoiling the flow of their design. The other option is to incorporate your shed into your garden design and make a feature of it. The best way to do this is to choose or design a shed that you like the look of, that you are proud to make a feature of your garden. If your aesthetic tastes are incompatible with your bank balance, you can always make a simple shed look nicer by using trellises to grow roses, or plant pots with climbers around the base, or you could consider installing a simple sedum roof.

Internally, the traditional potting shed set-up should generally have a propagating bench, tool and seed storage, large trays of compost and perhaps a loam mix. It is much nicer to work in daylight, so try to have a window close by so you can work properly. The best set-up, and the one I am most familiar with, is to have a propagating bench made from slats of wood with gaps between, then your large containers with compost and loam mix beneath. You can propagate or transplant your seedlings and simply brush the excess compost into the bins below.

It is a good idea to have your most frequently used gardening hand tools directly in front of you, hanging from hooks or pegs above the potting bench, along with storage boxes or a small set of drawers to house your seeds.

Seeds should be kept dry and preferably in the dark, either in their paper packets or sealed in jars. Keep plenty of labels and labelling pens at the ready; many is the time I have got to the end of my seedling day and completely forgotten where and what I have planted.

On another wall, think about creating as much storage as you can. It is a good idea to either have lockable cupboards or high shelving out of reach of children. Gardeners are notorious for using old plastic bottles, including lemonade bottles etc, as a means of storing highly toxic and positively non-child-friendly pesticides. If there are children around, all garden products, from weedkillers to organic growth supplements, should be treated with respect and stored carefully. After all, the ultimate aim of growing is to enjoy your garden and to relax in it.

By all means tidy your potting shed, but nothing will stay clean or perfect; you should give up on this idea early on if you want it to be a functioning workplace. Keep old wooden crates or potato sacks to store gardening hats, kneeling pads or thick leather gloves for handling roses or thorny shrubs. The garden tools and equipment that you use every day, such as the garden spade, fork, weeding hoe, hose pipe, watering can, clippers and trowels should all be easily accessible. If possible, your wheel barrow should be able to fit in all corners of your garden and this includes a route into and out of your shed. This way you can load it up with tools and pots and take it to the necessary area without making multiple journeys. A stone, clay or ceramic tiled floor is not essential but much easier to sweep out or dry off, I think of the potting shed as an almost semi-exterior place because of the way it gets used in all weathers throughout the year.

Another important building for gardeners is the greenhouse and it is becoming more popular to have a kind of potting shed/greenhouse hybrid. It is usually along the lines of a semi-glazed building with brick or wooden walls that has both plenty of glass and plenty of workbenches and storage.

Although you might struggle to grow some exotic species in such a structure, for most scenarios it is quite adequate. The greenhouse shed will save space by combining the two and the benefits of working in a pleasant environment with all your tools at hand is more than enough to compensate. Position your greenhouse shed as near to the open as possible to get as much sunlight and for as long a period as  possible. A stone path is best as you can hose it down thoroughly on those hot dry summer days and the moisture within will help keep your plants from drying out.

You don't always need to have a greenhouse to grow your seedlings, I didn't have one for years, but it's a good idea to have a cold frame if you can, either within your shed or outside. A simple wooden frame to house a tray of seedlings, with a hinged glass or Perspex lid, will allow you to air your plants during mild spring afternoons, beginning the process of hardening them off for their life as an outdoor species. Should the weather forecast an inconvenient spring freeze, your lid will provide enough warmth to save your carefully cultivated 'babies' from harm.

It may also be worth thinking about heating. If you are worried about temperature and it is possible to get electricity to your garden shed, this will allow you to use a low-powered electric heater on those chilly early spring nights. On my allotment, I would use an old paraffin heater – it was a sort of mint-green ceramic gas lamp which burnt a beautiful blue flame. It looked lovely but paraffin had already become quite expensive and using it was more costly than an electric heater, not to mention almost certainly more dangerous.

There is nothing quite like the look of a garden or allotment shed, its charm is ground deep within its well-worn, yet highly functional, walls. Its inhabitants all add character: a sack of potatoes chitting in a dark corner next to the apple racks; harvesting baskets and trugs filled with recently picked flowers and fruit. On the bench, a flask of tea, enamel tins with pumpkin seeds inside and a modest twig the perfect width for seed propagation. On the floor, casks and flagons and demijohns for brewing your favourite Sloe gin or damson wine. A garden shed is the king of sheds because within its walls we grow, we relax and we learn. If we are ready, the garden shed teaches us to slow to the same pace as nature, to smell the roses and to realise that all we ever really have in this life is the given moment and in that lies the power to be happy or not.

'All things are possible until they are proved impossible – and even the impossible may be only so as of now.'

Pearl S. Buck

CONTEMPORARY SHEDS AND SHED STYLE

The contemporary shed is what I have spent most of my shed-building days making for people. They are at the forefront of the shed revolution – the face of the brave new world of sheds. The modern shed is a wonderful thing, it is a place to explore our design fantasies, from unusual shapes or bold materials to new technologies or design innovation, it has none of the limitations of the traditional garden shed, so it can be basically whatever it wants to be.

In terms of design, the descriptive term 'contemporary shed' means very little. Fashions change in the shed world just as they do in others and any definition of 'modern' immediately develops the potential to become 'not modern' with the passage of time.

By using the designs and builds I have done recently as a reference point, I would describe the current perspective on the contemporary shed as an amalgamation of a few different design periods: the clean functional style of the Bauhaus period dating from the 1920s, mixed with mid-century modern and post-Second World War Scandinavian utilitarianism.

I would also include a sort of recycled version of William Morris, maybe because he is a personal hero of mine. A designer of extraordinary talent he is probably most famous for his textile designs inspired by the natural world, but his philosophy of designing and manufacturing goods that were affordable to most people rather than just the elite was a major influence on Walter Gropius, who began the Bauhaus movement.

The point I am really trying to make is that, when it comes to contemporary shed design, all styles are valid, anything goes. Don't get bogged down with what is on trend or what is old-fashioned, I try to look at an object or movement outside of time so I can see what is really good or bad about it. Contemporary sheds are about embracing the classic design ideas from our past, mixing them with the latest technologies and innovations and making them relevant to your own vision.

One of the most rewarding aspects of designing your own shed is the freedom you have. Your contemporary shed is your chance to try out those things that just weren't possible with your house. There is a multitude of options and remarkably few restrictions. If within your Victorian terraced house garden sits an eighteenth-century Japanese tearoom shed with a 1950s G-plan sofa against one wall, so you can project a film via your laptop onto the other wall, then this is modern design.

We usually think of our sheds as being symmetrical wooden structures, but there is no rule that sheds have to be square, rectangular or wooden – with the modern shed you do not need to be boxed in. Let the shape of your new shed fit the allocated space in your garden, let it sit on different levels; if you want to have a rhombus, a parallelogram or a dodecahedron, it is your choice.

Until recently, the urban shed builder seemed to be either stuck with a treated pine feather edge fencing, ship lap or a particular width of tongue and groove Western Red Cedar, all of which, I might add, are personal favourites of mine. These days you can choose to clad your shed in sheets of copper, mirrored glass, stainless steel corrugated iron or Perspex squares. Even the wood clad options have expanded lately, with Siberian Larch or Latvian Birch easily obtainable from semi-specialist woodyards. The reclaimed woodyards are especially interesting, although sometimes expensive, and some thick, old, battered sea defence oak timber, ripped down into cladding and placed next to a huge bronze-tinted glass window, is the type of juxtaposition that captures the spirit of the modern shed.

Probably the material which has most transformed the way we design now is glass. Our glazing technology has at last caught up with our aspirations, and sheds can now be flooded with light while staying warm and cosy. You can find toughened, self-cleaning, heat reflective and even smart glass (which, by sending two volts through it, can be dimmed from clear to opaque), and the cost of better quality glass has come down dramatically making it feasible to glaze large areas.

Glass is, of course, a two-way thing (disregarding for a moment our new friend the smart glass option), it allows us to see out, but it also allows people to see in. The trick is to allow light to enter where it will have the most

impact. If you have closed walls around your build, then put your windows in your roof; if you have no such restrictions, think about the path of the sun and put windows on the walls following this path.

The contemporary shed is often slick and sharp with clean lines and crisp edges, but not always. I find there can be a certain design hierarchy in some architectural circles, emanating from those who draw theoretically and aesthetically and don't fix bikes or smoke under cover in the rain. However, the modern shed can be unashamedly rustic; it is proud to be a Norwegian

cabin or Rocky Mountain shack and when you step through its doors it captures something of its owner that the sleek shed sometimes misses.

Perhaps a cider press sits next to a turntable playing post-Bebop jazz vinyl records from 1970s restored Warfdale speakers, or maybe there's a bar with craft ale on draught in one corner and a hammock for lazing in the late afternoon sun in the other (a particularly good combination, if you ask me). This freedom to create your own space and to indulge in your design fantasies is what makes the contemporary shed such a wonderful thing. If you follow fashion for the sake of it, then that fashion will move on and your shed will be old hat and so might you.

Another way of avoiding the sometimes sterile environment of the ultra-modern shed is to give your shed a story, try to put some history into the walls or floors or the objects within it. Use a mixture of old and new, put the modern right next door to the traditional and create a little drama. It is good design practice to create a textured theme as well as a colour scheme, perhaps plaster one wall and leave another in a polished pine or birch. It can also be good to give your shed a narrative. In the past I have used cladding made from locally sourced fallen trees; things like this create a talking point when people visit your shed, and it makes your shed more interesting and therefore more enjoyable.

What I love about the contemporary shed most of all is how I have seen it change people's lives, including mine. It has given people the freedom to express themselves in a way that they had not previously been able to do, by exploring their imagination with the design of the shed, but also exploring the ways they wish to spend their time.

CASE STUDY

The Man Temple
Approximate size: 9m²

The Brief

The concept of the Man Temple was to design a shed for meditation, one-to-one coaching and online Skype sessions. The shed was going to be situated in a narrow garden space that had a gradient. The shed needed to be bright and airy, with a sacred space for housing objects of spiritual significance, and it needed to feel compatible with its spiritual ambitions.

The Design

I remember the first discussions with the client Louis – there were a lot of ideas such as circular windows, unusual shapes and bespoke symbolic features, but the aspirations for the build were beyond the budget that had been set. Our initial meeting was essentially about getting to the core of what he wanted and simplifying it so that it was practical but still created the right atmosphere.

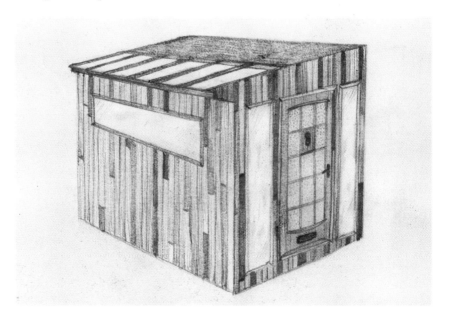

As Louis puts it: 'I knew I definitely wanted the place to be bright and I knew I wanted a sacred space that was peaceful, because I meditate every day. It was also important that it was not new and sanitised, it needed to feel right and have character. I have happy memories that come from the musty smell of sheds and garages, it brings back the feeling of being a child, young and free, but there is also something kind of masculine about going back to basics and being closer to nature.'

The build was to take the place of a decrepit old shed that sat in a darkened corner of the garden. The whole garden space was just 2m wide and around 12m long. It was an upstairs flat and access was via a metal walkway which joined the back door to the garden. In a space like this, the shed was going to act as a corridor, rather like a small version of the shipping container. My advice was to max out the 2m width, keep the shape as a simple box, but make it long enough to be multifunctional. The elements to prioritise would be a full-length roof window for light, reclaimed strips of different coloured cladding with an old door for character, a foldout desk and some bespoke shelving, including a low-level sacred shelf to focus on when meditating.

The Build

The build was the first of my build year and the weather was fine. As is so often the case in cities, the main obstacle was getting the materials through a house with no access to the garden, made worse by the fact it was an upstairs flat. This is one of the reasons I designed the whole build to be efficient on materials. An example of this is when I built the roof – it was just less than 4,880mm in length, which is basically just two uncut sheets of ply. The remainder of the roof width was made up of three pieces of glass to take it into a gutter. The gradient was an issue, so we levelled the back two-thirds and put the front on stilts to minimise the amount of groundwork needed. Cheaper feather-edge pine cladding was used on the sides and the back to keep the price down and since the front wall was so small it meant Louis could choose the cladding he really wanted and save some of his budget to get the interior right.

The Finished Shed

In a small space such as this shed, design basics come into play; keeping accessories to a minimum and well-chosen practical pieces of furniture ensure a clutter-free space. An old trunk doubles up as a table and storage, and a simple collapsible desk frees up the floor space for yoga. Light colours feel clean and reflect the light, and the simple natural texture of the wood helps make the space feel larger than it really is.

The ultimate aim of the shed was to provide a place that could be used for both meditation and for work. Although these are often at opposite ends of the spectrum, I think in this case the right balance has been struck especially since part of Louis' work is so intertwined in meditation. Louis agrees:

'Before the shed, I didn't feel as though I had the space to work from home. I now do loads of Skype sessions and I run online groups. I position the laptop so it faces down the shed, so you can see the space and people will always say, "where are you sitting? It's lovely." When I'm doing these Skype sessions I definitely feel as though I am able to go into a different dimension – sounds a bit psychedelic, but I really do. Sometimes I don't have the video on and I just sit here with my eyes closed. I know that no one is going to disturb me, I really go into a deeper level, I could never do that sitting in the house thinking that someone might disturb me or might be listening.'

One aspect that both Louis and I agree has worked even better than we thought, is the way in which the full-length skylights have really made the most of the natural light – it feels so light and spacious. This is all the more impressive because its location was previously considered a dark corner. It is so often the case that the building of a shed in your garden seems to give you more space than you previously had because every inch is being used and it also connects the garden space and the house with every corner of your garden.

With Louis' shed this extra space has gone a step further, as he reflects:

'One of the favourite things I did over the summer when it was nice weather was to go on top of the shed and watch the sunset, my neighbours were waving up towards me – this was a nice memory, it was beautiful. If I could change one thing about the shed I think I would have made some steps so I could get onto the roof more easily.'

Conclusion

What worked with this build was stripping back the requests Louis had originally and simplifying them. The shed is close enough to feel accessible, but separate enough to provide a new headspace. The 'luxuries' of the shed, i.e. the full-length roof window, the reclaimed cladding and door, and recessed shelving, have allowed the space to be practical while fitting the spiritual brief. It has succeeded in enhancing Louis' spiritual life and it has perhaps even opened doors of opportunity (as opposed to those of perception). Louis comments:

'One thing that happened here recently, I was asked to lead an online class with one of my favourite spiritual teachers called Ram Dass. He was professor of psychology at Harvard, part of the whole acid hippy revolution with Timothy Leary in the '60s. It was an incredible moment for me and it just felt so right to do it in this space.'

The world needs dreamers and the world needs doers. But above all, the world needs Dreamers who Do.

Sarah Ban Breathnach

'It is not so much for its beauty that the forest makes a claim upon men's hearts, as for that subtle something, that quality of air that emanation from old trees, that so wonderfully changes and renews a weary spirit.'

Robert Louis Stevenson

ECO SHEDS AND GOING GREEN

Eco can be a vague term. The word 'eco' is derived from the Greek for 'house' or 'place to live', but it is most commonly used as shorthand for ecological. The term ecological in fact concerns itself with the relation of organisms to one another but, in a modern context, the term 'eco' has developed a meaning which seems to change with the wind.

I have built sheds for people who believe that the very act of making something out of wood makes it 'eco', but if that wooden structure sits on a concrete base and is wired up to the house and is clad in a hardwood that has been chopped down and shipped from the Amazon Rainforest, then it is starting to lose its credibility somewhat.

Likewise, a contemporary-looking shed with clean lines and modern technology can harbour eco secrets. A structure built with sustainably grown wood, locally sourced doors and windows and high-quality solar panels can by stealth be doing wonders for the environment. But let us not be too mean or cynical about any of this, in most cases any effort made to be 'eco' is going to be a good idea and even philosophical intent can inspire a move towards a more ethical way of living.

In my experience, the most common perspectives on 'eco' lie somewhere between wanting to see and experience the garden, and wanting a shed to be built sustainably and act sustainably when possible. A good place to start with the eco shed is with nature itself. To be around nature and to be able to see nature can be fulfilling and relaxing, it doesn't matter who you are or what you do, everyone benefits from sitting quietly in nature.

An easy and simple way to be around nature is to start with some basic house plants. Over the years, I have worked on a selection of plants that I like to have around me, a mixture of good oxygenators to keep my shed air healthy and plants that will not die just because they haven't been watered for eighteen months!

The spider plant *Clorophytum Comosum* and Devil's Ivy *Epipremnum Aureum* are good at reducing air pollutants. Succulents such as the Jade plant *Crassula Ovata* and *Aloe Vera* can survive with very little water, especially in winter, and are also known for their ease of propagation, which equates to a free supply. The Snake Plant *Sansevieria Trifasciata* and Peace Lily *Spathiphyllum* are good oxygenators and will tolerate low levels of light; the huge variety of cacti are also worth considering for the same reasons.

Branching out from the house plant is a wonderful experience. On my shed I have gutters on the windowsills filled with alpines, I have hanging baskets and an old pallet on the wall filled with grow bags. Along the side wall of my shed I have raspberry bushes, a fig tree and jasmine creeping up to the roof covering the water butt and irrigation system. The allotment roof is another story all together, but the general idea is the more plants I can get within my view, the better I am going to feel and the better it is going to be for nature.

'Nature' the word is almost as difficult a concept to pin down as the word 'eco'. When I am discussing ways in which to introduce wildlife into shed spaces, I try to use the term biodiversity. It is important to recognise that if your aim in making an eco shed is to help nature in some way, then you should be thinking about biodiversity. After all, however important it is to save the planet, and it is important, it is also important to experience the nature we have around us in our everyday lives. The quiet and simple moments with nature are often the most rewarding and can provide a more intrinsic sense of well-being.

For this reason, I will not always keep my shed as neatly as others might do, which by coincidence fits perfectly with my adversity to tidying up in any shape or form. If you can keep your shed a little rough around the edges and, for that matter, your whole garden, in no time at all you will start to notice the changes. A few stacks of twigs, the odd broken tile or bricks, some scatterings of potted plants, will all provide shelters and homes for spiders, lacewings and even wild bees (which will attract more birds and so on to biodiversity). If you want to be more organised, use bird boxes, bug houses and even bat boxes or, best of all, introduce some water.

If animals are not your thing, it is perfectly reasonable to just make your shed and the area around it attractive, using grasses for dramatic foliage impact and plenty of potted plants or small potted trees such as bay, olive or ginkgo. There are many opportunities to build a relationship between vegetation and your shed: wisteria climbing the walls, summer tomatoes in hanging baskets or even a wall of moss. Maybe consider the green aspect of your shed right from the beginning of the design by having a living roof.

The living roof is an ecological big hitter. It backs up a green reputation with environmental benefits on all fronts. A living roof, as you may have guessed by the name, is alive. It is usually some form of sedum because of the soil depth, although it doesn't need to be. It increases biodiversity, improves air quality and can potentially be used to improve water quality. Having a living roof not only looks great, but it gives your shed the much talked about thermal mass – this means it retains some part of the temperature given to it by its natural surroundings. It acts as a kind of buffer to the weather and temperature outside. In summer months, the soil will remain cool and reduce the need for air conditioning. In the winter it will retain some of the heat of summer and act as an insulator which can potentially save a significant amount in heating your shed – all of this means you are using less energy, thus reducing your carbon footprint. This idea of creating an eco shed based on reducing the amount of energy it will require to run, can be just as rewarding as making it a home for nature. Of all the environmentally friendly systems that are available, the wood burner is perhaps the most rewarding. I am still often asked why the wood burner is good for the environment, the basic principle being that when burning wood, although we are releasing the carbon the tree has, this carbon will be released anyway as it decomposes. A wood burner can also get your body moving. The famous quote attributed to Henry Ford springs to mind: 'Chop your own wood and it will warm you twice'. These words were actually mentioned by Henry Thoreau at least 60 years earlier in Walden, and Thoreau attributes the quote to a man with a team of horses who was helping him clear stumps from his bean field.

The act of chopping wood into convenient-sized logs that will fit your burner and heating some soup on your potbelly stove is definitely eco, but it also feels eco. I can vouch for the fact that there is nothing quite like sitting in a shed you have built, with the wood burner firing and working all day knowing that you have been completely sustained by your shed.

Of course, once you have created heat, it is a good idea to stop this heat from escaping – this is most successfully achieved with insulation. Insulation may seem obvious, but it is so often the one element that is neglected. I started my building experience in loft conversion and the rules and regulations surrounding lofts meant that good quality insulation was always something I took for granted. Without insulation people soon realise that once their little wood burner goes out, the shed turns chilly, fast. In my experience, it is often the case that you don't always want or even need to light a fire for heat, and the addition of good quality insulation in your build will mean you can use a small heater for short periods, or even rely on the heat of your body and appliances.

The area which shows the most potential to change the way we use energy is perhaps solar power. Solar power is not only sustainable and non-polluting, but it is also indefinitely renewable, or at least until the sun dies out. Harnessing the sun's power using a photovoltaic system becomes more efficient and more widespread every year. A 2015 study showed the price per kilowatt dropping by 10% per year since 1980, and predicted that solar could contribute 20% of total electricity generation by 2030.

I have a cheap and simple set-up. I bought my solar panel second hand for a ridiculous price and it charges a couple of leisure batteries which are more able to cope with the fluctuations of recharging. With this I run some simple 12 volt lighting. Solar-powered LED lighting is a great way to get you started, it's simple to set up and because the lighting is low power, you

should always have enough juice to keep your shed illuminated even in a country as sunlight challenged as the UK.

There is a recent gusto for making new things from old and this is great, but recycling or upcycling does not always have to be rehashing old broken pallets, of equal importance is just using the stuff we already have. It can be as simple as not throwing away your granddad's desk and fixing the drawer with some wood glue. This is recycling at its best and it adds a bit of history and a bit of soul to your shed.

Recycling is cheapest with your own hands because correcting inconsistencies or adapting purposes can be quite labour intensive which costs money. Recycling is also not always possible or desirable, but this doesn't mean you don't have an ethical choice to make. If you prefer to go down the new materials route and want to be true to your eco ethos, then it is worth knowing where your wood has come from.

Sustainable wood comes from sustainably managed forests. This means that the forest is managed to prevent damage to the environment and wildlife by taking a long-term view of the trees as a resource. The point about buying from sustainable sources is that timber is consumer led just as every other product is, so if you buy ethically, you are also avoiding the support of illegal deforestation. Generally speaking, softwoods are more sustainable than hardwoods simply because they grow faster and are more easily replaced.

The EU has introduced legal measures to protect its woodland and forests. Because the law limits annual harvesting and places a minimum requirement on replacing harvested trees, buying wood grown in Europe is usually a good choice. Wood from Asia, Africa, South America or even North America, currently comes with fewer guarantees but the only way to be sure that what you buy comes from well-managed, sustainable sources is by looking for the Forestry Stewardship Council (FSC) logo. The FSC is an independent, not-for-profit organisation promoting responsible management of

the world's forests. Their certificate system provides an internationally recognised standard-setting and trademark assurance to any business or individual who is interested in supporting responsible forestry.

My shed won the Eco category of Shed of the Year, before going on to win the top prize in 2014. I have quite a love of the outdoors and nature, so my perspective on the eco shed reflects this. Whatever your perspective, my suggestion is to try and be respectful to nature in some kind of way, it doesn't matter how small. Have some plants, don't be too obsessively tidy, leave some places for insects to shelter and survive the winter. If you

like nature and you are concerned about the environment, why not use your shed as a reason to try and do things with the environment in mind. It might turn out to be a little more expensive, but money spent ethically can seldom be considered a waste. What is money after all but an attempt to put a value on the things around us and if we do not consider the protection of the environment to be a thing of value then human life surely loses its meaning.

CASE STUDY

The Brief

The concept was to create a shed that provided a micro environment for wildlife, particularly for invertebrate creatures to hibernate in over winter. It also needed to act as storage for the equipment used at educational events. It was predominantly built from recycled materials, including the leftovers from a recent barn restoration. The shed was built for the Berkshire, Buckinghamshire and Oxfordshire Wildlife Trust, and was commissioned by Lynn, the Education Manager.

The Design

The project was a collaborative one in which we combined our various expertise regarding wildlife, natural habitats and shed building to find the solution. Lynn explains the ecological premise:

'Over the last 20 years or so wildlife organisations, including the Wildlife Trust, have been encouraging people to provide more crevasses in their gardens because we have become too tidy. One of the methods which has come about to try to achieve this is to create what has come to be known as the bug hotel, which involves using things like old bricks, piles of old pallets and stuffing them with lots of different materials so there is a heterogeneous micro environment for the invertebrate life, particularly for creatures to hibernate in over winter. This creates those types of habitat that would have existed naturally in the past and are increasingly disappearing.'

I had seen various versions of the bug hotel online, but none as big as the one we were going to build. The shed would basically be a 2m cube and we decided to split the build in half, separating the front and back. The back half would be a conventional shed with a simple door. It didn't need much more than this as it was primarily to avoid carrying a class full of nets over the field ready for pond dipping. The front half of the shed would be designed to provide shelter

for as many different kinds of wildlife as was possible. The size of the front needed to fit the dimensions of two stacks of large pallets.

Geographically the shed was at the far end of an expanse of grass known as Fox Field. It was close to a pond and it made sense, both aesthetically and for wildlife, to face the shed towards the pond. Since the primary objective in terms of the wildlife was to create a safe place to hibernate, there was always going to be the need for a roof to keep the inside dry. I suggested a living roof, first because it would sit in its surroundings well, but also because it would act as an insulating layer by which the thermal mass of the earth would regularise the temperature more than a conventional roof thus helping the wildlife. The design for the interior would be largely organic depending on the various materials that would become available from around the site, but there were some definite ideas based on a knowledge of which type of creatures lived in the area and what type of habitats they would prefer.

The Build

I had help building the shed from Dan who also worked for the Wildlife Trust. He had some good ideas on how to provide the best habitat for the creatures we were trying to attract. Since the shed was in the middle of a large field, the only way to get power over to the site was to use a small generator. It just about managed enough power for the chop saw to cut, but we had to turn it off when not in use to save petrol. The build is burnt into my memory because of the heat. We built the shed in the height of summer on the hottest week of the year and since we were in the middle of a field there was no shade whatsoever. Besides bringing as much water with us as we were able to carry, there was a water source in the next field and I remember hosing myself down like an overheated horse at lunch times. I actually wore shorts on the first day of the build and burnt my thighs, so I built the shed in my pyjamas because they were the only long trousers I had with me.

We started the build in the usual way by concreting posts into the ground and making a frame. We used a damp-proof membrane and filled it with old bricks, tiles and rubble beneath the floor base. The idea was to create a hibernaculum that would be suitable for creatures to crawl into, especially the amphibians from the pond. We purposely left access holes that larger wildlife might potentially be able to use. The framework went up fast, with the majority of time being taken up in constructing a simple pitched roof. After this it was all about getting a variety of materials on site so we could decide how we were going to put together a mansion suitable for wildlife.

The shed was predominantly made of recycled materials from the grounds at Woolley Furs – the main site. Materials such as logs, pallets and old bricks were easy to come by partly because there had recently been a refurbishment of a large barn on the grounds. We found some left over butyl liner and protective fleece, which had been used to make the pond, and we used this as part of the living roof. I had constructed a strong roof with a good amount of depth and the large sods of grass we took out to make the base were packed tightly onto it.

We made as many different habitats as possible knowing that some might work better than others. We had managed to get a decent quantity of sheep's wool from the livestock manager and we packed the centre of the shed with this to give it a warm heart. Next we stacked around 20 pallets in two rows on top of each other and started the long task of filling them with various sized logs and lengths of bamboo. When the logs were in place we drilled different sized holes into their front face. The drilled logs and lengths of bamboo were designed to house queen wasps and hairy-footed flower bees, which crawl into the holes and seal them up to hibernate through the winter months. The holes were drilled at an angle so that any rainwater hitting the face of the mansion would be inclined to exit.

Next we built a sort of mini dry stone wall in the hope of providing a home for tawny mining bees and red mason bees living in the area. We used a mixture of old bricks and small paving stones, and drilled holes in them to simulate a decaying wall as this would be more wildlife friendly. We then used small plant pots, stuffed them with straw and fixed them into place on the pallet upside down so they were protected from rain but had small access holes at the front for lacewings to crawl up into and hibernate. We also found some wooden grills and fixed these into place with more of the black sheep's wool behind – the idea being that some creatures, perhaps spiders, would crawl into the gaps or larger wildlife might use the sheep's wool for nest building. Finally, we clad the front apex underneath the roof, purposely leaving gaps for wildlife to crawl into and we especially left a long downwards facing slit which we hoped might be accessed by bats seeking a home.

The Finished Shed

As we walk across the field to see how the shed has fared over the years, the naturalist comes out in Lynn and she instinctively examines some droppings within a few metres of stepping outside. She points out badger sets and describes the current scent-marking battles, she explains why the heat of the compost heaps attracts the snakes and she reminisces about some heron sick she recently encountered next to the pond that had five undigested newts in it and a partly digested greater water beetle. Apparently, some birds will vomit to get rid of the weight to allow for a quick getaway. As we approach the shed it looks just as I remembered it, perhaps better than when it was first built because it has weathered into its setting. The imperfect yet structured layers of various objects and materials look like something nature would have designed. I suppose it is easy to overlook the aesthetic value the shed has. Lynn views it in a similar light:

'I think it looked more beautiful than I expected it would. I said that at the time, you made it look beautiful rather than just a bunch of stuff piled together, because these things usually don't look that attractive. It's a lovely backdrop to the activities that happen here. The pond is often used for pond dipping by families, so inevitably there are photographs being taken and the shed in the background makes it look more beautiful.'

What really matters to the Wildlife Trust and to me is whether the shed is successful in terms of providing a home for nature. The hope was that Mini Beast Mansion would successfully house invertebrates as it had been designed to, but there were a few pleasant surprises that Lynn revealed to me:

'As you can see, these bamboo shoots have been all bunged up by bees and there is something that comes and pulls out the wool, probably for a nest somewhere. I've always wondered what it would be. The pond is chocker with smooth newts. We couldn't possibly know unless we lifted it to do a proper survey, but I imagine it has done a lot for the population of the amphibians. The stoat was something we didn't expect, we knew it would be a fantastic habitat for invertebrates but that moment when we saw a stoat dive under the shed was really exciting because we hadn't thought about anything like that living there. From a nature point of view, the only thing we're not sure about is the bat entrance to the eaves. A bat specialist said it is probably too low, but there are definitely butterflies using it to hibernate in winter, I have seen Red Admirals and Peacocks in there.'

Conclusion

I found the whole experience of building this shed rewarding, partly because it was lovely to physically be around nature in a field and partly because there is definitely an unexplainable happiness when making something that will exist for the benefit of wildlife and the teachings of nature. The shed is a success both in terms of its practical use for storage and its use as a habitat for invertebrates, perhaps even overachieving in some regards with the discovery of the stoats. The most common mistake when constructing these things seems to be the lack of a roof, since it is the roof which keeps the creatures dry and safe through the winter but also stops the whole structure from rotting in a few years. The benefits seem to be quite wide-ranging and Lynn summarises it better than I can:

'Fox Field was a far duller place before the shed was built. The whole area has been enhanced over the last few years, not least with the shed. But the real enhancement is the stuff we can't see easily because it's going on at a different scale, both in terms of size and time to our own human time scale and that is all the toings and froings of the invertebrates that use it. The shed has made the area better on many different levels including one which is outside of the human dimension.'

'All human evil comes from a single cause,
man's inability to sit still in a room.'

Blaise Pascal

RELAXING SPACES AND THE SHED SANCTUARY

There was always a modern world and it was always advancing to a place
beyond our natural state. Our current 'modern world' is not harder than
past generations, but the technological advances are increasingly taking
away the opportunity to sit quietly and spend time with ourselves. The shed
as a sanctuary is not a new phenomenon, but it has a new resonance in a
fast-moving, technologically advancing, social media-filled existence. Our
ambitions have us marching towards progress, but if our idea of progress is
material gains, that separates us from the simple, more meaningful things in
life. The value of peace has never been greater and the shed is becoming the
place that generates it.

In the sanctuary shed, silence is enough. It works best when the TV,
the laptop and the iPad are replaced with books, a comfortable chair and
a teapot. In my hours of peace, I allow myself the luxury of music and a
reading light – in a shed of sanctuary there is nothing wrong with luxuries. I
think of Clouds Hill, the tiny shed-like cottage of T. E. Lawrence (of Arabia
fame) where he sought to escape the intense scrutiny of his celebrity status.

His famous quote, 'Give me the luxuries and I will do without the essentials' is a comment on the time he spent there.

I am guessing that you are not living the restless life that follows returning home after leading an Arab Revolution against the Ottoman Empire, but nevertheless, the necessity for an escape, all be it from everyday domestic chaos or a recent contagious bout of overtime at work, is an important one.

For most of us, there is a peace in nature, a place routed in looking outward both physically and emotionally that gives us a sense that the world will carry on regardless and that our problems are ultimately just thoughts that will at some point leave us. If you can bring some of nature to your shed, then you can bring peace with it. Simply being able to see garden space from your shed window can provide enough sustenance to change your state of mind. Even the use of basic materials such as wood and metal, natural fabrics like cotton, linen and muslin have a surprisingly satisfactory effect on the senses.

Our ideas of peace and sanctuary are subjective and the influence they have on the shed is wide ranging. Some of us appreciate the low-lit snug style of a country pub, an armchair next to an open fire, with dark wood surrounds and a sleeping family dog. Others prefer the clear natural light of a yogic retreat, with clean air and swept floors and space, lots of space. Surround yourself with things that are familiar, that make you feel you are at home or, better still, create the home that you imagined for yourself. The details are important; it should not be a place you feel physically uncomfortable in or a place in which your body has to work hard to stay warm.

It is better to be aware of your thoughts, you should move away from the idea that shed sanctuary means a place to hide away, avoid the idea of a place to sit and cower from the world, think of it more as a celebration of rare solitude. Consider having a day bed or if you meditate, perhaps install an east-facing window (in the northern hemisphere) for your morning mantra. Equally if evening is your time, picture yourself having a last cup of tea as the sun sets through a west-facing porthole.

As when making a workspace or creative space, separateness is everything. Get to work on relaxing, and set up your shed space as homage to all that modern life has managed to squeeze from the human condition. Your shed is the place where you are allowed to feel yourself and be with yourself – the self that existed before your burgeoning online presence, so don't overcomplicate matters. Use a straightforward layout, with simple stripped-back furniture or basic materials such as bare wood and undyed leather. What is the purpose of life if, after all your hard work and efforts to be what the world expects of you, you cannot also have a place in which nothing matters – where you are allowed to be you.

I return to Clouds Hill (below) for my parting thought because it summarises the way in which a place can be an expression of how a man sees the world and an attempt to find the peace within. The simplicity of his retreat was everything to T. E. Lawrence, nothing was considered superfluous – there was somewhere to rest, somewhere to read and somewhere to listen to music. He bought, borrowed or built the simple furniture and fittings himself, it was a combination of the bareness of his life as a tribesman and the fruits of classical civilisation which he held so dear. Above the door inscribed in Greek is *Ou Phrontis* (Why Worry), the meaning of which lies in understanding the transitory nature of life and finding peace with it. In his own words Lawrence deftly sums up what a sanctuary shed is all about: 'Nothing in Clouds Hill is to be a care upon the world. While I have it there shall be nothing exquisite or unique in it, nothing to anchor me.'

'No man is an island, entire of itself; every man is a piece of the continent, part of the main.'

John Donne

ENTERTAINING SPACE

What we have in this world becomes meaningless if we cannot enjoy it with others. The solitude of a quiet cabin should be broken on occasion to warm walls and warm hearts. It could be that your shed will open up to others once in a blue moon, it could be that you want a shed for the very purpose of cultivating gregariousness.

When I think of socialising in a shed the first thing that comes to mind is a good single malt, indeed a bar is quite the tradition in the shed world and a good way to introduce others to the most beautiful of all the experiences of life: daytime shed drinking. Personal habits aside, it is good to be social, it makes the shed experience better if other people can enjoy it.

I have built extravagant bar set-ups and they work well in a shed, but a small elbow height surface is enough get a keg of your favourite draught ale on tap. Often I will integrate shelving into one of the internal walls behind the bar so you can easily secure a small collection of spirits with optics and have a decent amount of space for a drunken glass. A sloe gin can sit beneath your bar top or even a nice looking cupboard can be sufficient to arrange your bottles of choice, and a homebrew hiding inside will appreciate the peace.

Eating is the other great social event of the friendly sheddie. Summer kitchens and BBQs built into the shed or the porch are an easily accessible way to get cooking and a sensible way to cut down on the massive dishwashing haul of a family meal. I have noticed it is much more common to have at least some basic cooking facilities outside in America and other parts of Europe than it is in the UK, probably due to the unpredictable weather. Herb plants are a good choice for any outdoor kitchen area, they smell wonderful and picking a sprig of thyme to cook with on the BBQ makes the whole experience a more enjoyable one. As day turns to night and that single malt makes an inevitable appearance, lights are needed as the eyes adjust. Candles

are better than bright lights at this point, or if you're lucky enough to pick up a good gas or oil lamp you can recreate the atmosphere of an older time.

A porch comes into its own in entertaining shed scenarios, especially if the doors of your shed can be opened out to make use of both the internal and external space. Best of all is to have at least some kind of cover over the front porch area to shelter under in an emergency. If you're planning to use your shed for social gatherings all year round, then you may want to think about a chimenea or an outdoor gas heater, and the use of anti-slip finishes on your porch when the colder wet weather arrives is sensible.

One thing people don't often think about is the ability to change spaces easily. Sometimes we get obsessed by trying to fit all the stuff we need into a shed, we forget that if a space changes we may not need so much stuff and it is often the flexibility of a space that determines how useful it is. Foldaway benches, lift-up beds and stackable seating will help your shed adapt to different scenarios, and don't forget wheels – even the heaviest of tables can be swiftly negotiated into a corner if it is put onto heavy-duty caster wheels.

We also want a bit of both worlds, to be with our friends sometimes and to be alone at others, and the ability of a shed to transform itself into

what is asked of it is perfect for the entertaining shed. Maybe a projector can drop from the ceiling for a weekly film night, the floor space can be cleared to make room for a ping pong or a fusball tournament, or that wheelie table can be locked into place to house the turntables for a middle-aged man party.

Clutter doesn't work all that well in the entertaining shed, other people don't tend to understand your own stuff. If you can keep the sentimental trinkets to a minimum there'll be less sentimental breakage. The mess of a social shed gathering can wait until the morning if need be; with sheds you can take a more relaxed attitude to the guests. Give your guests some space to move around in if possible, you don't want to be clambering through garden tools and stepping over extension leads to get another beer or slice of apple pie.

If the main focus of your shed is going to be entertaining, you may want to consider the folks next door, nothing spoils a party like a disgruntled neighbour. If you have the option, you can keep the doors facing away from the least favourite of your neighbours, but often you don't really have this luxury in a tight urban garden space. In such cases, think about using a high-density plasterboard and when the evening comes you can move people inside to carry on the party.

Sometimes we can get so bogged down in making something right or in trying to create perfection that we forget the purpose of our lives, and an entertaining shed can remind us. I remember the times with other people in my shed with equal affection to the time spent alone. Ultimately it doesn't matter if your shed is finished perfectly or if it will add value to your property. Life moves fast and what truly matters is that we spend time with our family and have some fun with our friends every so often.

'If you cannot do great things,
do small things in a great way.'

Napoleon Hill

SMALL SPACES, BIG IDEAS

Sheds by nature are small and shed life is all about understanding limited space since, more often than not, the ambitions we have for our sheds are greater than the space we have. It is design that comes to the rescue, and a mixture of the practical and the imaginative will help any shed's spatially challenged cause. The space we have, or rather the lack of space we have, is not always the problem – most of us consider small to be a negative, but what matters is the way in which we organise our spaces and the way in which we perceive them.

The amount of space needed for a specific shed can change dramatically depending on the type of use it will have. For example, if you intend to fix bicycles in your shed you are determined by the length of a bike and the space needed to easily work around that bike. If you are going to use it as a writer's den, then it is possible that all you will need is a comfortable chair, some kind of work surface and a laptop or other form of writing machine. It is perfectly possible to run a business with the same equipment as the writer's den, with the addition of a high-speed broadband connection.

What is not possible is to reduce the size of a bike, since it is not possible to reduce the size of a human, or at least not significantly enough to make the small bike workshop practical. The trick is to recognise which areas of your shed you are able to enhance and which you are not, so you can make the most of what you do have.

Dimension is also important in small spaces. Apart from the obvious conclusion that a larger dimension helps, different shapes can be more useful for specific purposes. The front section of my shed is a modest 7m², the dimensions of which are around 1.8m x 4m. At this width, the space acts as a kind of corridor so only one wall can be used for a desk and a workbench, but for the purposes of artwork and writing this has worked well for me. If the space were 2.7m x 2.7m it would be roughly the same footprint size – I would have a smaller workbench, but a larger useable floor space and I would have potentially three useful walls instead of one.

If you cannot change your footprint size because of garden limitations, then you may want to think about going higher than your local permitted development restrictions – this will involve getting planning permission, but if you succeed, the extra height can transform your space. Extra height makes a shed feel more spacious and with a little imagination it can also provide extra useful physical space. You could think about hanging a hammock on the roof rafters or building a raised mezzanine for a small bed or, if space is very tight, even a small bookshelf is going to help you to keep your main area tidy and efficient.

The creation of extra space can be taken a step further by using the area on top of your shed. My shed has a garden roof. I use it more than my actual garden, because it is so high it gets wonderful sunlight and I'm able to grow things I can't on the ground. With a small shed in a small garden this can be invaluable – there is literally no space loss, since the footprint now exists on top of the roof.

It is critical with smaller sheds to try and maximise physical space, but it is also important to increase the sense of space. The use of light colours, which feel clean and reflect light, and simple natural textures help make the space feel larger than it really is. Another way to deceive our perception of space is to connect shed interiors with their external environment. Skylights or large windows work so well because they are making the most of natural light, but they are also drawing your eye outwards to your garden. In the same way, doors that open out onto decking or even large steps can make a space not only feel bigger, but on good weather days, can allow your shed life to easily spill out onto the porch and if you design your shed to have a decent roof overhang then even the weather need not be a problem.

By far the most successful way to achieve internal order is to consider storage early in your design. I would normally say around 20% of a room should be designated to storage. The temptation with a small space is to decrease this, but, in fact, it can be sensible to increase the percentage.

Storage comes in many forms; shelving is often the first port of call and understandably so. Bespoke shelving can be designed to perfectly fit your own reference books or storage boxes. Bags hanging from hooks and pegs are a fun way of using the walls for storage while staying flat to the wall.

Tables and chairs can be designed to store things underneath, long box benches with lift-off cushioned lids are especially useful or an old-fashioned suitcase is a good-looking and practical way of providing both a coffee table and storage.

The creation and use of space unites all the sheds in this book. The benefits we gain from the creation of space are dependent on how well it is designed to fit its purpose. This is more complicated than just an ability to pursue a certain task, what makes good design is that we can pursue that task with ease and enjoy it. One of the main reasons a shed becomes less enjoyable to use is the accumulation of modern clutter. When I am designing a shed for clients, after a short, polite probing into their lives, I often find that the primary reason for making a shed is either to create new space in which to put 'things' or to make a new space to be free of 'things'. In larger sheds, it is possible to accommodate overspill from the house, but the smaller the shed, the less successful this is going to be.

The best tip of all I can give when trying to maximise a small space is to make it efficient; this means stripping away the dead wood and understanding what it is you genuinely need in life. If you can keep only the essential, practical and meaningful objects around you, your shed will function far better.

Perhaps it is time to sharpen your tool kit. At some point in your life you realise the importance of the acquisition of good quality tools and the benefits of keeping them in good shape. Whatever work it is you are doing, one good quality tool can do the work of many bad quality tools and so reduce your clutter. Tools come in many shapes and sizes. If your tools of the trade are for fixing bikes, then choose Park Tool Torx keys or a set of Teng ratchet spanners; if you are illustrating children's books then choose top of the range Cannon or Epson scanners and printers. Spend time making these decisions and budget this equipment into your whole shed build early on, so you know you can afford these things.

This chapter has mainly focused on how your limited space will be better if it is tidier. At this point I feel the need to confess, because the way I use my limited shed space is far from minimalist. I know the rules about space and more often than not I agree with them, but my life has not really turned out like that. I'm quite suspicious of the phrase a tidy place is a tidy mind, especially in a creative environment, like a superior mind confirms to the rule of tidy law. I have chosen to have things around me, my stuff makes the space feel like mine, you could not mistake my shed for anyone else's, and it is filled with things from my past, things that inspire me. I admit that there are some strange and perhaps 'useless' sentimental objects around, but my mess is mostly made up of a mind-boggling amount of what could loosely be termed as 'tools' – from airbrush compressors to a selection of chromatic mouth organs, to a box filled with various Vespa scooter parts. It is a sort of contradiction, but the freedoms that I now have in my life are made possible by all this stuff. They have allowed me to work for myself, to keep my expenses at a minimum and to be relatively self-sufficient.

I think what I am trying to say in all of this is that to understand your limited space, you have to understand yourself. I know roughly what I am – I am creative, thrifty, practical and sentimental and this sometimes manifests itself in a form of hoarding and mess. The challenge I have in my life is how to avoid my shed becoming a junkyard, but I can manage this and for me it is not worth losing the gifts I have in life in order to achieve this.

More and more I find that when I am designing a new shed, it is not just about the aesthetics, it is about the person; it is not just about making the shed fit a space, it is about making it fit a personality. The goal in designing for limited space should be to simplify, but simpler does not always mean less stuff, it is about living a simpler life and understanding what is meaningful to you.

> 'Happiness doesn't depend on what we have, but it does depend on how we feel towards what we have. We can be happy with little and miserable with much.'
>
> W. D. Hoard

TINY HOUSES AND BEACH HUTS

Tiny Houses

Space is, of course, relative – what is small for some is not so small for others, it just depends on how you perceive the space. Some sheds are small in size, but big in concept. One growing movement that embraces this ideal is that of the tiny house.

The tiny house movement is both an architectural and social movement, originating in America. It is generally considered to be a home of 500 square feet (46m²) or under, as opposed to a build of 1,000 square feet (93m²) or under, which is considered not tiny, just small!

The tiny house movement is primarily a vehicle to downsize, but crucially it is motivated by a belief that living a simpler life will help to provide a more enriched and fulfilling existence. The general principle being that by reducing mortgages or becoming mortgage-free, we are able to work less, enabling us to spend more time with family or pursue tasks we care about rather than just the acquisition of money.

The tiny house makers are usually concerned with leading a less wasteful and more sustainable life, often using a mixture of recycled construction materials and modern technology to keep their bills to a minimum. Part of the movement is also about getting back to nature. The builds are often photographed in the wild picturesque landscapes of America, but the opportunity to construct in these places is, of course, subject to the acquisition of one's own land and the permission of local authorities.

A way around this obstacle has been to make the tiny house mobile. The tiny house on wheels is often built onto the frame of a large trailer base, should the time come to go on a road trip or even move home, the house can be hooked up to a large vehicle and away it goes. The moveable tiny house is an extension of the recreational vehicle or motor home culture and, if built properly, these modern houses will outlast the vehicles used to tow them. The tactic of moving your home is useful throughout the world. Often if a build is moveable, it is classed as a non-permanent structure and, as long as it is moved from time to time, it can be a useful way of creating a liveable or useable space on your land when planning permission is denied.

Variations of these types of homes have, in fact, existed for hundreds of years – shepherd's huts and Romany caravans, for example, have historically navigated the continents. The re-interpretation of this nomadic lifestyle has made use of both modern technological advances in appliances

and the ability to generate money using the Internet. Regardless of technology, the essence of the moving home will surely endure until the end of human civilisation.

Many of the tiny house designs have similar principles to other small dwelling spaces such as caravans, barges and boat cabins – using composting toilets, gas-powered showers, multipurpose kitchen sinks and foldout beds and work surfaces. The recent surge of interest in the tiny house movement probably came after the financial crisis of 2007–08, when the more affordable and ecological lifestyle became an attractive proposition for people who had lost their homes due to repossessions or for those who were now living in negative equity. Both the fixed and the mobile tiny house communities have continued to grow in recent times, partly because of TV coverage but also because of how these builds are now viewed socially and culturally.

The attraction of a place exempt from building regulations that is relatively easy and cheap to construct and provides a lower cost of living for those with no savings has very few negatives. Add to this an ability to tailor the space to any environment, so it is ready to be rented out on Airbnb, and it's easy to see why the concept has been embraced. Certainly, the tiny

house movement is showing no signs of slowing and whole communities are beginning to move towards self-sufficiency. Recently, the first tiny house-friendly town was declared in Spurs, Texas.

The philosophy of the tiny house and its undoubted links to minimalism is something I have great admiration for. The idea of living small, of decluttering and simplifying routines, relationships, thoughts and an attitude to life is something we can all learn from.

Beach Huts

It is difficult to explain the British beach hut to everyone. Stories of freezing cold summer days, of sand scratching wet skin, clothes being thrown off before running into the sea and how the smell of a post-dip hot chocolate promises to make the world safe before the drive home are lost in translation to those from warmer climes. Like the garden shed, it is an ordinary and wonderful place filled with cold wood and memories of happiness.

Far from British shores, early beach huts existed as far back as 1862 in the form of bathing boxes at Brighton Beach in Australia as a response to the Victorian morality of the age where the ruling classes preached sexual restraint, even if they didn't practise it. The modern notion of the beach hut evolved from these wheeled bathing machines used by Victorians to 'preserve their modesty'. The purpose-built early twentieth-century beach huts were regarded as holiday homes for 'toiling classes' but by the 1930s attitudes had changed and the hut's image was somewhat revived. With the advent of the Second World War, all British beaches were closed along with the huts, but the end of the war saw a resurgence of the humble hut and the 1940s and '50s are considered the British beach hut heyday.

The modern love affair with the beach hut is driven by a certain amount of nostalgia, but fuelled also by people realising the value of these little huts by re-imagining the space. The beach hut is no different to the shed in that it is a place where you can express yourself and one which you can alter to fit your own needs and tastes. Few of us are ever able to live permanently by the water's edge and privately owned huts in desirable locations are famous for commanding high prices, but who can say this 8m² gem is not worthy as it sits just above the high tide mark of a childhood beach, sheltering families and looking out to sea in all weathers – the source of hot drinks, tangled kites and treasured memories.

'The wiser course is to think of others when pursuing our own happiness.'

Tenzin Gyatso

GUEST ROOMS

The guest room shed is a close relative of the tiny house. It is often the build that gives you an extra room in your house and is, in effect, the cheapest way to increase the area of your property without paying for an extension or a loft conversion. If your guest room is built the way you want it, then soon enough it will coax you from the safe monotony of your house and lure you into using it as your summer bedroom, because to be closer to the garden is to be closer to nature and a more peaceful and relaxing night's sleep.

One of the most popular builds I am asked to do is a shed that frees up the seldom-used spare room so it can be converted either into an office or a baby room for a new arrival. Indeed, for so many, the spare room is a schizophrenic amalgamation of bedroom, office and dumping ground, and the main issue regarding the new shed is to not export this unfortunate burden out into the garden. The creation of a guest room shed is your chance to throw out anything that is not going to be useful and design something with purpose.

The freedom and uniqueness of this shed means it is a favourite of the teenager, due in part to its separation from the house, which avoids the irritation of investigative parents. Its use as a bedroom for family members extends to older children who return home so they can save for a house of their own, or as a simpler form of granny annex for ageing family members visiting more often to see grandchildren.

To make a shed useable as a bedroom takes more work than the creation of an office space or work shed, and this is true right from the start. Most sheds do not need planning permission if you stay within local guidelines. It is, however, much more likely that a shed built for sleeping in is going to require either permission from planning authorities or the involvement of building control, or both. It may help matters if you explain that the build is for a family member since most authorities are more concerned with rogue landlords making large sums of money from unsuitable or poorly maintained housing.

The summer months for the British garden guest room are easier than the winter months. If you intend to use the room all year round, it is sensible to budget in quality insulation and draught proofing. You may also want to use a mixture of different heat sources – a wood burner can be cosy and atmospheric but if quick heat is required then include an efficient electric heater. Although your guest room shed is different in atmosphere to your home, you are attempting to reproduce a similar level of comfort to your house.

A dual-purpose shed is often the most useful as, in many cases, relatives or friends will be periodically visiting and it would be a shame for the space to be otherwise redundant. When it comes to sleeping arrangements, for versatility I prefer a decent sofa bed, so you can have your floor space back when people aren't staying. You could also construct benches that come together to make a sleeping surface or a foldout wall bed, either way I always suggest getting a good quality mattress to iron out any carpentry shortcomings – less sleep should be the last compromise of life.

As always, storage is essential. If you do have a bed, make use of the storage underneath it. This doesn't mean squeeze every homeless object you own in there, but it is useful to try and have a bed high enough for your guests to easily stowaway their suitcase and pull it out again. A simple chair next to the bed makes getting dressed and undressed easier, and provides a place for shoes and clothes for the next day. Practical elements such as foldout ironing boards are things that are not only going to be useful, but also give your guests a sense of control over their life, and simple things like installing a wall mirror will help your guests feel good about themselves and happier as they step from the wilderness and back into society.

Ideally, your guest shed should be self-contained. The addition of a small bathroom and toilet will set it apart from the work shed, and will also

avoid the awkward midnight stumble through the rose garden. A 15m^2 build is plenty of space for a self-contained bedroom. For example, if your shed is 5m x 3m, I'd suggest a 1m x 3m bathroom at one end of the build, separated by an internal wall with a doorway in the middle. This is surprisingly useful and adequate space to put a shower one end, a toilet the other and a small sink opposite the bathroom door entrance. You could also consider curtains and half walls, but walls do offer those little moments of privacy that can be gold dust when away from home.

Tiled bathrooms are ideal, although it is worth considering the warmer surfaces of marine ply or modern non-slip vinyl. When it comes to a kitchen, it is surprisingly easy – the most difficult part is the kitchen sink; like the bathroom, you will need to coordinate with a plumber to get your hot and cold water supply. After this a small fridge and a two-ring hob is enough to make simple meals. If you don't want to get this involved, an area for a kettle and a teapot is still nice, perhaps even essential if you are British.

Try to think of the shed more like a hotel; this means keeping the place spotless and providing clean towels and toilet paper – people like a change of environment, they seldom enjoy a change in hygiene. It is also worth considering that if your shed guest room is going to be a special place then your relatives may never want to leave. The quality of build you achieve is a matter for your own conscience and is most commonly affected by your compassion as a human being and the distance to the pub.

PART 3

BEFORE THE BUILD

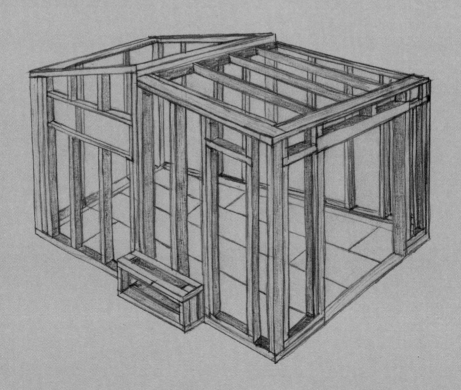

'Having knowledge but lacking the power to express it clearly is no better than never having any ideas at all.'

Pericles

FROM IDEAS ON PAPER TO PROJECT BEGINNINGS

Making a Drawing

By now you will have a good idea of what you want to achieve with your shed. If the shed is multifunctional, then make a decision about its primary and secondary uses. You may have lists of possible features and bookmarks of images that inspire you, but until your shed exists all of this is theoretical. It is time to act on these ideas and move towards making your dream shed a reality. Start making some sketches, rough drawings are a great way to get a feel for your shed. Sketches can also determine whether the proportions you have chosen look right or if you like a specific design at all. For these reasons you should try to draw well so here are some of my suggestions to get the most out of the process.

When making sketches, the larger the piece of paper the more freely you will tend to draw, so choose A3 rather than the back of a cigarette packet. Markers or soft pencils will give you softer lines and free movement, which are useful for understanding ideas early on in your design. Although it is good to draw freely at first, as your ideas move on try to also draw with purpose, emphasise the beginning and the end of your line so that your image has conviction. Use scale and guidelines to check the proportions and try not to use a rubber; the guidelines will give the sketch character. Don't be afraid to start again, it can be better than over adjusting.

Do not try to draw in perfect detail from one end to the other of your page, instead begin with the general shape. When you are happy with the design then work on some of the finer detail and if you find yourself focusing in one area, step back and analyse the overall look to see if you are still on the right track. If you render a drawing in with light and shade, it will help to convey the mood you are searching for. Fine-point pens or harder pencils have a more definite feel and they become more useful when the design approaches its goal.

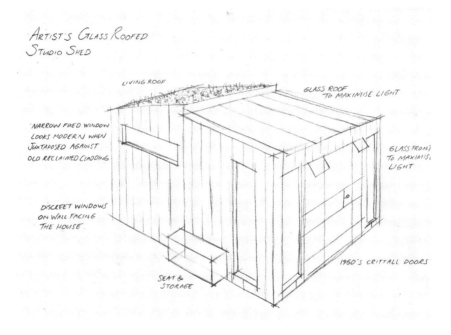

Artist's Glass Roofed Studio Shed

LIVING ROOF

GLASS ROOF To MAXIMISE LIGHT

NARROW FIXED WINDOW LOOKS MODERN WHEN JUXTAPOSED AGAINST OLD RECLAIMED CLADDING

GLASS FRONT TO MAXIMISE LIGHT

DISCREET WINDOWS ON WALL FACING THE HOUSE.

1960's CRITTALL DOORS

SEAT & STORAGE

Computer drawings tend to be used to give specific detail. When overused or used early on they can stunt the creative process with clinical geometry or the endless options can overcomplicate matters. If you are making a three-dimensional drawing and it is difficult, then imagine it cased in a geometrical box, then draw the shape within that box; it will help you break it down into manageable shapes that are to scale. A model might also be useful to understand the three-dimensional space – a simple cardboard cut-out is going to be best to help you make decisions because it can be changed easily; any detail in your model making is going to be of little use until your design is definite.

It is good to make an accurate plan of the internal footprint to understand the amount of space you have. If you have specific items of furniture that will be used in the build, perhaps a sofa bed, a large workbench or a washing machine to be situated out of view, then make scaled cut-outs of the furniture so you can move them around your floor plan. Scale models of interior pieces will help you organise the internal layout and make sure everything fits, they will also help you to see circulation pathways so you can understand how you will move around your shed. I would also say that if you are struggling with ideas then just start drawing anything, soon enough you will get in the flow, and ideas and structure will eventually come.

BASIC DESIGN PRINCIPLES

It is going to be useful for you to understand some of the principles of design, because to learn from what already exists is a way of having hundreds of years of experience at your disposal. This information is going to give you the tools you need to make good decisions and make your shed design a better one.

Over the years I have studied various concepts and ideas about design and architecture. The shed is different from most other building design because of its size and its individuality. While many processes and concepts involved in designing a building become more important in a small, individual space, others break down.

I am a builder and a shed user as well as a designer, so I am able to navigate between an idea or concept and how to build it. I have used this experience of working between the different fields to distil and simplify architectural theories into the ten basic design principles that are most suited to the designing of a good shed.

A Central Idea

It is good to have a central idea that brings the whole shed project together. It should exist in the shed's DNA and it will galvanise connecting ideas, as well as giving you direction and focus. It seems to be the case that in modern thinking the idea of being objective shows a higher level of understanding than being subjective, but this is your chance to be subjective in life, since the shed is an expression of you. The more specific the idea you have, the more successful it will be. If you try to make the shed something that everyone will like, it can become diluted and not suit anybody. With your shed, you do not have to conform, it will be more interesting if you do not and other people will probably appreciate it more because you haven't. When you think you understand the central idea of your shed, give it a name – this will energise the design and make the whole process more focused and more enjoyable. Perhaps your shed will be a place to escape, in which case you could name your shed 'The Sanctuary'. Or perhaps, like my 'allotment roofed shed', the way the shed will look or function can inspire its name.

Relationship

By relationship, I am not talking about how you are going to talk your other half into allowing you to build, because then this would be a book of infinite proportions. Design is the relationship between what will exist and what already exists, and good design makes the two things compatible. Your shed will probably sit in a garden or outside space next to a house. Whether or not it reflects the style of the house or is in contrast to it is not the issue, it is that your shed knows the house is there – it has a relationship to it. This is true of the garden also; you should understand the garden as a place you move through in order to get to the dwelling space of the shed. If you understand everything within the build in terms of its relationship to where it exists, then the build will become more connected. A door

handle is part of a door, a door is part of a wall, a wall is part of the shed, the shed is part of the garden, and the garden is part of the district and so on. For example, something simple like using leftover cladding to make a desk will connect the interior with the exterior.

Function Creates Form

The way a design looks is the result of the most suitable way to build it. The proportions of a shed are decided by the space available and the most suitable materials with which to build it. For example, a cottage-style shed exists not because the people who built cottages wanted it to look like a cottage, but because it was the best way to build a shelter with the materials they had to hand. The quaint, small cottage windows are a result of the small panes of glass that were available at the time and designed so as not to let too much warmth escape from the building. This is true of modern design also. For example, a flat roof design is primarily due to the 2.5m height restriction of a shed and the chunkiness of the look is because of the thickness of the joists needed to span a particular length. Good design will understand the function of a build first, then marry it to the aesthetics. It doesn't work as well the other way around, especially in smaller spaces.

No Dead Space

Space is everything to the small build; ultimately what's important with design in small spaces is to reduce dead space. This is true externally in terms of maximising the footprint, but it is also true internally in terms of the placement of objects and pathways. Design with intent; imagine the space being used for the purpose it was intended and in this way it will function better and the dead space should be reduced. Simple clean routes of movement through your shed will usually give you more practical space and will avoid creating areas that are seldom used.

Multipurpose

A multipurpose space will be more flexible, more functional and will act as a bigger space. For example, a table that can be wheeled or a desk that can be folded away to make space for a floor mattress creates space that otherwise would require two areas to achieve these different uses. Design solutions are often more effectively achieved by the connection of different elements and you should therefore try to have multiple reasons to justify a design choice. For example, a window gives you light, and it may also frame a beautiful view of the garden; if you place a desk in front of a window that gives you both the light to work and a good view – multifunctional.

Balance

Balance is the key to making a shed function well and look great. Externally, asymmetrical form is considered more sophisticated, but this is only true because to balance asymmetry sometimes takes more complex forms. We do this quite naturally and it needn't be complicated. For example, a door placed in the middle of a shed front could have two equal sized windows either side of it to make it symmetrical. A door placed on the left side of the shed front would have a larger window built on the right side to balance the asymmetry. Balance can use opposites as well as equals and this can enhance certain aspects of design by creating an aesthetic counterpoint. So, a busy wall of shelving becomes more interesting in clean space, a rough texture is exaggerated next to a smooth wall. A wall or space will also feel more balanced when it is split perpendicular to its longest length, this could be achieved by using a painting or shelving to split a wide wall from top to bottom or floor tiles with their longest side laid on the short axis of a room.

Less is More

Keep things simple. I am not talking about minimalism or creating a sterile environment, but if you have a long list of features to include in your build, choose the best ones and go all-out to achieve them. A shed likes a focal point, but don't make it a TV. Choose one feature to focus on: a wood burning stove, a workbench or a wall of shelving. Don't over design for the sake of it. The shed is different from a house, you are in control of how it will be because it can be designed from scratch, you can make any quality of the space real. If you want the space to feel light and airy, then have a large window and large doors as opposed to just painting in certain colours. If you want it to feel strong and substantial, you don't need to pretend – use thick timbers.

Everything Has a Scale

Because of the small size of a shed, scale is exaggerated – a rectangle becomes a corridor and a square becomes a box. The proportions of the things within your space should be in proportion with the build itself. Good art and design reveals different things from different distances. Your shed should also have a pleasing proportion from far away and interesting detail close up, and, just like a painting, a building can lose something if it is overworked. When choosing objects, whether accessories or a workbench, consider the scale as a whole – do not go too dainty and do not choose things that are going to physically overpower the space and make it difficult to use.

Rule of Three

Colours, textures and forms work well in a shed with a rule of three. Choose three colours: the first should be 60%, secondary 30% and the last accent colour 10%. Rules are meant to be broken, but it's useful to consider this balance so they are not fighting with each other. This translates well to materials and texture also. For example, you could have internal walls of plaster and wood cladding with copper used as an accent. Similar percentages related to the golden ratio can work well with external proportions and when splitting up the internal space. The rule of three can also be a useful reference point for finishings, such as lighting or artwork.

Be Authentic

The shed is your space and ultimately there are no rules except that you should be true to yourself. Being authentic doesn't mean being what others think of you or what you think you should be. Being authentic is being yourself and making a shed that expresses this.

Artist's Glass Roofed Studio Shed

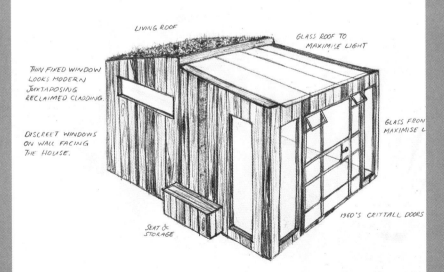

LIVING ROOF

GLASS ROOF TO
MAXIMISE LIGHT

Thin Fixed Window
Looks Modern
Juxtaposing
Reclaimed Cladding.

DISCREET WINDOWS
ON WALL FACING
The House.

GLASS FRON
MAXIMISE L

SEAT &
STORAGE

1960'S CRITTALL DOORS

CREATE A DESIGN BRIEF

Following on from the Inspiration section of the book which hopefully flooded your head with ideas, now would be a good time to create a design brief. A simple breakdown of what is required will enable you to focus ideas towards your goal of achieving your perfect shed.

Write down all you have learned so far. The purpose of your shed and what will make it function properly. If it is multifunctional, put the functions in order of importance. The approximate size of the shed – include the height, width and depth – and should this size change, then write down the parameters within which you are allowed to build. What your budget is and if you have a contingency budget. When you would like the shed to be built: what time of year is best and over what timescale? Write down what you already have – perhaps the base is already in place, perhaps you already have materials you can use – and consider what kind of labour you have at your disposal. Bear in mind the overall shed style you like, both internally and externally, and your definite dislikes or don'ts regarding the project.

Do not set these plans in stone at this point – they are just a guide, something to ponder over or a base to build from, things will probably change. If it is the case that you already have a good idea of what you want to achieve and you have a strong concept, then this is fine also, but at the same time try to stay open to new ideas and don't be afraid to throw away a great idea if it is not going to work or if a better one comes along.

Artist's Glass Roofed Studio Shed

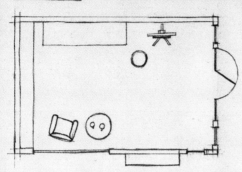

Features

- Living Roof
- Glass Roof
- Fixed Windows & Crittall Doors

Interior

- Shelving for Artist equipment
- Artist's Workbench
- Room for Easel & Stool
- Comfortable chair & coffee Table.

Artist's Glass Roofed Studio Shed

Design Brief

Size: 4.2m × 3.2m   **Budget:** £10k

Purpose: To create a light and airey artist's studio for painting.
In keeping with a mature garden space.
Warm enough to use all year.

Function: Primary: artist's studio.   Secondary: storage and relaxing space.

Style: Modern, eclectic, vintage, reclaimed.

Notable Materials: Reclaimed hardwood cladding, glass, steel doors.

Absolute Wants: Living roof, reclaimed cladding, crittall doors, lots of light.

Definite Dislikes: UPVC plastic, interior darkness, out of place in garden.

Understanding Cost

The cost of a build can be difficult to accurately estimate. There are lots of variables based on aspects such as size, shape, quality and who's going to do the building. It can also be difficult to decide how much you want to spend on a project.

In very general terms, it is common to pay roughly the same amount in materials as you would in labour, but obviously this fluctuates with the area in which the build is taking place and the types of materials being used. If your design requires a high-level finish, then you should be prepared to spend as much on second fix as you will on first fix. In terms of the whole build, the finishing or bespoke elements may allow the space to function properly and should be valued accordingly. In the later stages, it may seem as though the build is slowing but this is not necessarily the case. You will see more visual progress when the build is getting framed out than when your bespoke shelving is being made because you are paying for the extra time it takes for more intricate work.

The amount you spend on labour is determined by who is doing the work. There are good and bad builders because in all industries there are good and bad workers. A good builder is worth a good amount of money. The building trade sometimes has a bad reputation because of unethical builders, but it can also be the result of clients who are not willing to pay the right amount for a job. If you are asking a builder to do a job you are not willing to do yourself and not paying them properly, perhaps it is time to re-evaluate your opinion of work.

If you can do the work yourself, you can potentially save a decent sum, but this is not always possible. From my own perspective, I happen to enjoy labour exchange – it brings equality to the workplace; since time is the truest of all our resources in life, it is a great leveller. I also enjoy using clients or architects who want to work for me, because they realise how physically difficult and skilled the job of building can be.

The amount you spend on materials is partly determined by the size and design of the build and partly by the quality and availability of the materials you use. Standard building materials – such as treated pine carcassing, OSB board and plywood – will not fluctuate in price as much as some of the more individual items – such as cladding, doors and windows – but in both cases, it is worth shopping around to find bargains. It is wise to consider second-hand items because they may be of better quality than a newer version for the same price, but it is important to factor in the labour costs needed to make second-hand items fit your build. It is also useful to think ahead if buying second hand, for example if you find some nice wooden doors before the build starts, the framework can be built to accommodate them.

You should design what you can afford to build, but only after all cost solutions have been exhausted. By this, I mean be creative. It is often the case that you think you can't afford something, without realising that a cheaper version may be viable – for this reason it is good to have alternatives to designs aided by research and imagination. This is the key to good design – anyone can have ideas, but making the ideas a reality at the right cost is the true skill. It may also be worth stretching your budget; I often say to my clients, you are already spending a good amount of money on your shed, if you need to spend a little more to get what you want, then do it. Spending money is not necessarily a bad thing and spending more may be more cost effective. For example, you may win later on the cost front if the quality of work is better or the work needs less maintenance. It is also the case that you shouldn't necessarily spend

money just because you have it. Before the build starts you should secure the estimated cost plus at least a 20% contingency. The aim is to have money to spend, but not money to waste.

Although a good quality shed can add value to your home, the shed is your chance to think outside of economics. To understand this perspective, it is wise to remind yourself of the difference between value and cost. A bespoke build is something that is made for you and it therefore has a greater value because it will give you more enjoyment. The shed is not a commodity; it is a way of life and if it helps you change your life into something that was better than before, then it will be good value for money.

Before you consider building your shed, take another look at your design brief – re-evaluate its purpose and the costs and do not hold on too tightly. A good designer is not afraid to throw away good ideas for the sake of what the build needs.

PLANNING PERMISSION AND BUILDING CONTROL

One of the first considerations when embarking on any build is whether you will need planning permission. The initial question appears to be quite simple and you might expect a 'yes' or 'no' reply. However, it can be more complicated than that. The safest guideline is always to assume you do need permission until you determine otherwise, as it can be an expensive mistake to build something and then be told it has to come down.

First, you should not confuse 'planning permission' with 'building control'. Planning permission is the consent required by law to build on land or to add to or alter the use of existing buildings. Although this description refers primarily to the UK, most countries will have their own variations of these planning laws.

Planning permission in the UK is now governed under the Town and Country Planning Act 1947. However, the rules do change and are controlled by local planning authorities, which in turn are usually overseen by local district boroughs or councils. Although the planning rules are covered in the planning portal, councils and planning officers often interpret these rules differently. Generally speaking, planning permission is about the look, the size and the position of the build.

Building control/regulations are the minimum construction standards by which buildings are allowed to be built. All buildings will usually come into this category unless the building is below a certain size – usually a floor area of 15m². However, there are many other considerations apart from size that affect whether building control will be needed. Building control is also concerned with the quality of the materials, insulation, fireproofing and structural integrity.

If your property is within a conservation area or a designated national park, it will almost certainly need planning permission, and such a location will often mean that there are more rules affecting the design, usually to keep the external look of the build in keeping with its surroundings.

In many cases planning permission is not needed, for example buildings of minor or insignificant development (which usually includes sheds) fall into what is called 'Permitted Development'. This in turn carries its own set of criteria and may still require 'building control'.

Garden buildings in the UK are generally considered to not need planning permission if they stay within the following rules:

- a single-storey building with a maximum eaves height of 2.5m and maximum overall height of 4m with a dual pitched roof or 3m for any other roof;
- if within 2m of the property boundary, the maximum height of the build is not more than 2.5m;
- it is less than half the area of the existing original garden or land surrounding the house;
- it does not contain a sleeping area.

A full list of criteria can be found on the UK government's Planning Portal. However, it is always wise to consult the local planning department for advice and no charges will be applied if permissions are not needed.

There are some common misunderstandings of the rules that come up from time to time when I'm talking to clients. For example, the term 'temporary structure' is often used, but it is not really applicable since a temporary structure is considered to be a structure that would be in one place for less than 28 days. However, it is a useful definition for mobile sheds or tiny houses. Sometimes people assume either the architects, planning consultants or builders have some responsibility regarding the rules around permitted development, but ultimately it is your responsibility as property owner to consult your local planning department.

Remember, you should not necessarily be put off from applying for planning permission, although it will almost certainly cost you money. Planning can be the difference between getting the build you want and making do with what you are allowed, and this can have a significant effect on your shed's functionality and value. An example is a music studio I built in London. Originally, the studio was going to be built within permitted development, but for the extra cost it took to get it through planning, the studio height was increased to 3.5m. The studio shed was designed to be used as a professional mastering studio and this extra metre in height completely transformed the acoustic properties of the build, allowing it to function properly and enabling it to generate more money in the process.

CASE STUDY

The Hackney Studio
Approximate size: 25m²

The Brief

The brief from the client, Olly, was to create a recording and engineering studio shed that could be optimised sonically within the confinements of the space it was being built in. The studio needed to have a high level of soundproofing because it was going to be built next to a hospice. It was also important that it be a good environment to work in with plenty of light and be finished with bespoke elements to give it an individual character. It also needed an element of storage for garden tools.

The Design

The design for this shed was predominantly focused on using the right dimensions and materials to optimise the sound qualities of the space and to make it as soundproof as possible. A decision on the dimensions was influenced substantially by using Bob Gold's room mode calculator (which can be found online). It is quite a technical concept, but the general principle is that soundwaves have a length and at certain points as a wave bounces back from a surface it will have constructive and destructive interference. By altering the dimensions of the room you can manage this interference and create a more sonically neutral space. The walls of the studio were designed to angle away from the mixing area to avoid standing waves, which are soundwaves bouncing between parallel walls; a similar principle was applied to the ceiling by using a gradient.

The shed has one large window facing the garden, one in the roof for light and two small windows for cross ventilation. The sound insulation was achieved by using layers of sheep's wool, acoustic sound boards, dense matting and various decoupling methods throughout. The garden tool storage is a sheltered corridor to the rear of the build.

Ultimately writing and mixing music is how Olly makes a living, so the quality of the build needed to be of a standard to make his work easier and potentially better. Given he would be spending long periods

of time in the shed for his work, the space needed to feel comfortable and enjoyable to be in. Getting this balance right was to some degree theoretical since previously he had been used to working from a small room in the house. Olly was clear about his motivation for the build:

'Working in the house was far from ideal sonically; a tiny room means there is a lot of guesswork and mixes become a little hit and miss. In terms of making music, building a shed studio is a no brainer. My wife has done very well to put up with me; when you're making music you listen to the same piece of music over and over again a hundred, thousand times, so me getting out the house was not only going to be better for her, but also for me as I'd be not so self-conscious. There was also a certain romanticism attached to the idea. My dad built a simple shed at the bottom of his garden in Devon. I once took my studio down, or part of it, it was a fun couple of weeks. I guess that always stuck in my mind and made me think it was possible.'

The Build

The build was a challenge and I would say the physical effort it took was underestimated. It was quite a large building for a small team to build and to make matters worse all the materials had to be lifted over a 9ft brick wall at the back of the garden. The amount of materials it takes to construct a building of this size is substantial and was further increased because there were so many layers. For example, the wall structure of the build from inside to out was: 18mm ply, two layers of acoustic sound board, 4in x 2in carcassing, another layer of 18mm ply, 2in x 2in insulated gap, another layer of 2in x 2in air gap and a final layer of 18mm ply. I can remember one day personally lifting over 100 sheets of sound board over the brick wall.

The build also took longer than expected. This was partly due to the lack of access and the size, but also the amount of soundproofing and decoupling. Internally there was a high density acoustic membrane by Tecsound throughout, followed by resilient bars and genie clips to decouple two layers of sound board from the framework of the build. There was a thick semi-floating floor that consisted of sound board, a thick rubber matting and a layer of plywood over the floor and half the wall space. These

various layers all took time to construct, but were necessary if the studio was to be soundproofed to the standard Olly wanted, and decisions on quality also extended to the detail of the aesthetic finish:

'For better or for worse, everything was pretty bespoke. That was partly down to naivety, but I also needed a certain shape and soundproofing because I didn't want to disturb the hospice next door. You have to decide how much it is worth it. I am pretty uncompromising by nature, but there is a decreasing marginal utility on expense, when you spend extra money it might only make it 5% better. If you have all the money to spend then it doesn't matter.'

The Finished Shed

As I stand in Olly's shed now it is easy to conclude that it was all absolutely worth it. It is acoustically advanced and it has a high level of soundproofing, but what immediately strikes me is just how wonderful a space it is to be in – it feels bright, it feels spacious and the shed manages to balance its functionality and form perfectly. Olly concurs:

'The design isn't 100% purely for function; it would probably be better on paper if it didn't have windows but it would be a hellhole to work in. The window opens all the way out which is great in the summer because it gets really hot. Sometimes I'll be working in boxer shorts, which is one of the perks of having a home studio. Everyone who comes in here is immediately struck by how lovely it is, including the cat. For some reason, he loves to sleep on the keyboards; he has this comfortable sofa to sleep on and he doesn't bother.'

Externally, the shed manages to connect to its environment and looks impressive without being imposing. The bespoke, careful finish of the cladding, windows and doors give the shed a sense of the craft that resonates with its ultimate purpose. Indeed, the reclaimed cladding softens the edges and makes it feel as though it has been in the garden for years. Internally, it is good to see that the plasterwork has been sealed and left rather than painted; in its raw state it is suited to the raw materials of the plywood and wooden windows that surround it. You can also see Olly's hand at work in here which makes the shed better – more personal. With a little bit of help he put together the industrial-looking lights with vintage bulbs, and the diffusers which look amazing:

'I love the lights. Although the Edison bulbs are an un-eco friendly way to heat the studio, they look great. I justify it because they are a good heat source. I also have a 100% renewable energy tariff, but eventually I may put solar panels onto the roof. I also like these diffusers on the wall, they turned out great. Everyone thinks they're a piece of artwork but they perform a sonic function. They work well on that wall; that space is designed to be reflective and a bit lively, opposite the dead end which should be neutral for mixing.'

In terms of the acoustics, Olly is also extremely happy with the build. He has finely tuned the sound of the room with careful positioning of various diffusers and acoustic panels and, given the relatively confined area in which the studio had to be built, the initial results were surprisingly consistent with what he had expected:

'In a smallish room, managing the interference is always going to be an issue and given the calculations from the shape of the build, I knew this issue would be at around 37 Hertz and sure enough I have a bit of a boost here. This is a long-term thing and I'll make a little resonator to absorb this wavelength in the future. After my research, it's interesting to see the theory come to life; the room doesn't feel like a mathematical formula but sonically it is very predictable. The one thing I didn't predict is that there is a road about 100m away and 37 Hertz also happens to be the resonating frequency of an idling bus at the traffic lights!'

Conclusion

This studio shed is definitely one of the more impressive-looking sheds I have built. Although there were time issues regarding the build due to the access and size, and Olly admits he may have perhaps overdone the high-quality bespoke elements, from my perspective it reflects his nature. His attention to detail is one of the reasons he is good at his job and to his credit he was always patient and we worked well together. The resulting finish is beautiful and ultimately the extra time and effort has made the build more special. The studio is already working well, but the fruits of our shed labour are perhaps yet to be realised. Olly is excited about the future:

'I've never had a situation in my entire studio life, that I've had a representative monitoring system. When I hear a sound coming out of these speakers, I know that is what it really sounds like. That's just a revolution for me, usually I'll be working in extremely imperfect environments and it's a bit of guesswork. It's nice having a sonically neutral space, but it's also such a lovely place to work in, there's a really good vibe. I think the effects it will have will be profound over time and it will hopefully reflect in the work that comes out of here.'

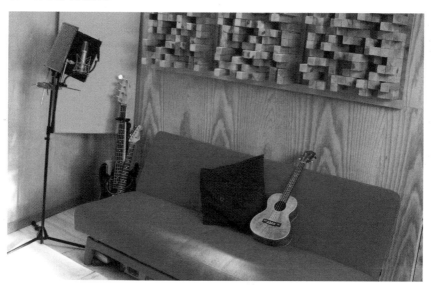

BUILDING RELATIONSHIPS

If you are making a shed on your own, the act of building can be a contemplative experience. It can also be physically difficult and take a very long time. Reducing build time means acquiring extra hands, and when other people are involved your shed build immediately has to deal with relationships. Relationships are an important and often neglected part of any building process and, by using different specialists on your project, you are potentially gaining more knowledge and expertise – but this can lead to different opinions. You may want to coordinate with electricians, plumbers, waste removal, or with solar panel or wood burner fitters. The involvement of these various trades is usually a relatively pain-free experience, but frictions can arise if mistakes are made or there are significant delays. To reduce the potential for disruption, an understanding of who will be doing what and when it will be done is crucial. Remember, if someone is good at their job they will usually be busy, so book early.

Most of the time, specialist trades will be working for a small portion of the build time (depending on the complexity of the job), but you should be in contact with them early on to avoid complications. For example, you may want to talk to an electrician even before the build starts to know the source of power or to understand the possible implications of having lots of appliances in your shed. Or if you are having a wood burner fitted, you should discuss installation methods because it may impact the roof design.

It may be the case that you wish to involve an architect. A good architect can be many different things, but the essence of the job is to decipher the information they are given and balance it with their own vision so as to design the most suitable build for the space and the personality of their client. Finding a good architect is difficult, in part because sheds are often a small project and as such it is not always economically viable to use them. However, it is not just about the money, as in any walk of life you are going to get the best results when you can find a person that not only has the experience but also the desire to do the job.

Usually, the most important relationship you have will be with your builder. A good builder is often many things; in fact, they often need to be many things to translate an architect's theoretical ideas. They should be someone who knows how to produce a quality build on schedule by efficiently understanding plans and transforming them into practical build solutions. Finding a good builder can be difficult because without the builder there will be no shed and this means they are often booked up in advance.

The problems in a build usually arise from a miscommunication between the client, the architect and the builder. In my experience, this miscommunication takes place because of presumptions made about each other's various roles and a wish to protect their own positions should something go wrong. The best way to deal with this is to get everybody in the same place at the same time to define their roles, and to create a positive atmosphere from the outset.

There are times when people just don't get along. I can remember moments when I had to refuse to build something because it would have been dangerous and the architect stormed off. In these scenarios, it is sometimes best to just decide which people you work the best with or if someone is being unreasonable find a replacement.

All of this matters, because relationship problems will not only impact the cost and the time it takes to complete the build, but can sometimes generate resentment towards the building. Avoid viewing the whole building process as a transaction, whereby you pay someone to complete a task.

Everyone who is involved in your build will put a little bit of themselves into your shed. If you can respect their work and be grateful for it and show them, this good feeling enters the soul of the building, not only because the people involved will be more inclined to do better work for you, but also because the atmosphere of the build will remain in your memory.

BUILDERS MERCHANTS AND SPECIALIST SUPPLIERS

Buying building materials can be difficult for the building novice. There are so many choices each with their own cost variations and claims of superior quality – at times it's hard to know who to trust or how to make a decision. Just as with the building process, my advice is to break up the building into a series of digestible categories and then get to work on finding each material, and soon enough it won't be as complicated as it first seemed.

There are those among us who will enjoy carefully working through all the variations, but for those who don't, either because you would prefer not to be involved or because you would prefer to focus on the act of building, then as part of your negotiations with trades you can ask either your architect, project manager or builder to do the ordering for you.

Either way, the benefits of deciding on materials early are substantial because the materials will inform the way in which your shed is built and this knowledge will make things run smoothly and will therefore save you money.

To choose the right materials, you should think about your budget, your work schedule and your aesthetic preferences. Having established a preliminary budget, work out what materials cannot be compromised; knowing how much money is left will help you decide on which finishing materials to choose. There are three routes to sourcing and buying all the materials needed. You can select a good 'supply all' builders merchant, go it alone and source materials separately from specialist suppliers, or ideally take the middle ground and do both.

Most large builders merchants will have a local branch, offer free deliveries (sometimes with a minimum order) and be competitive on

price for general run-of-the-mill products. I will generally use my builders merchants to supply me with the materials to build the shell of the shed, which usually consists of: concrete and 4in x 4in posts for the foundations; a tongue-and-groove floor structure; 4in x 2in wall structure; 6in x 2in roof structure (depending on the roof size); OSB board out; breathable membrane; 2in x 1in batten out and 18mm plywood for the roof. I will  also often include the insulation and the plasterboards in this initial order.

If you do decide to use one supplier you should consider your access to the build – the materials will be delivered by a large vehicle and either craned or lifted off by hand and put next to the property, if you live on a tight road it is worth mentioning it to the supplier as they may be able to send a smaller vehicle. Often there are more materials than you might imagine and this means storing them until they are needed. So, you need to consider the workspace in your garden and understand your work schedule; it might be worth splitting the order into two or three parts to keep things tidy on site.

As the build gets more bespoke, the suppliers will become more specialised. Cladding, glass products, doors and windows, specialist timber and roofing systems all have many variables and budget – availability and aesthetic preference will define which materials to use. I have various specialist suppliers that have provided me with a good service and I will use them consistently but, since personal tastes can be very specific, I will often suggest that my clients do their own research if they require a specific material or to find the best price they can.

Small independent suppliers can be useful especially if they are local to the area; they will usually have smaller dedicated vehicles to deliver smaller amounts of materials at regular intervals. If you order from a supplier locally it also gives you the option of picking up extra materials if the order you have made is not sufficient. There is nothing worse than being short on cladding and having to pay a large delivery charge for a few pieces to come from the other side of the country. Local suppliers will also often have a good knowledge of local planning rules. For example, some local authorities insist on certain types of insulation or have regulations on smoke emission reduction from wood burners.

When calculating orders for either building the shell or for the cladding, it is quite standard to add a 20% contingency. This is to account for the loss of the material due to offcuts or even mistakes. Obviously you should try to keep mistakes to a minimum but they do happen and it is better to order a little more than you need rather than lose time or have to reorder.

If you do decide to go it alone and order from different suppliers based on cost, it is important to factor in the time needed to do this research and coordinate deliveries so they arrive on site at the correct times. The logistics of coordinating different materials from a variety of companies can be considerable and it may not turn out to be as efficient as you first imagined; ultimately, this is what paying for a project manager or ordering from a single supplier is trying to avoid, but if you plan your build early there is no reason why you cannot make it work.

Whatever buying option you choose, good negotiating will definitely be useful. Discounts are always available if you know how to look, but often it is just a case of asking for a trade discount. Never rely on a single quote for expensive products, but do always compare like for like because the cheapest isn't always the best.

Always ask advice on anything you are not sure about, suppliers will have manufacturers' reps who are only too willing to give advice on the use and technical performance of their products. Try to get samples where possible as there is no substitute for seeing and testing products, especially in finishing materials such as cladding and ironmongery.

I would also just add that it is ok to have your own opinion and that you don't need to be talked into buying a certain product. The more information you get about the materials you want to use the better, and more often than not suppliers will be helpful. However, if you feel you want to do something a certain way or use a certain material then do the necessary research and have a go.

A MESSAGE TO THE SELF-BUILDER

It is simply not possible for everyone to build their own shed, as you may not be able to get the time off work or it may be physically too difficult for your body. However, if the reason for not building is that you don't think you can or you don't know if you will enjoy it – think again.

There is nothing quite like the feeling of being in a place that you have constructed from start to finish. When I look around me, I have the memory of fitting the wood burner, ripping down the logs to make cladding, lifting the soil bucket by bucket up a ladder and onto the roof, even in little things such as the hook on which I hang a small mirror, I can see my hand at work.

There are lots of aspects I enjoy about my shed, but ultimately what makes it special is that it is mine and it feels like mine because I built it. I want other people to experience this feeling too. It is difficult with larger builds because few of us ever get to the position of wealth or experience, never mind the physical strength, to build our own house. The idea of self-building may be daunting and you may not feel qualified, but you should remember that the building of shelters is something that is intrinsic to humans and it is something we have done since civilisation began.

To build your own shed, some basic building knowledge is required, but not as much as you might think. Most of the essential information is regarding structure and since your structure will primarily be built from wood then a good knowledge of this material is going to help. Even experienced carpenters can misunderstand wood or take it for granted. Sometimes in life, the things we are closest to we often overlook and because we are around something every day we presume that is enough.

Let's start with a definition – wood is a porous and fibrous structural tissue found on the stems and roots of trees; it is a natural composite of cellulose fibres (which are strong in tension) embedded in a matrix of lignin (which resists compression). This short statement about wood already provides us with enough information with which to build properly, but I think it is easier to understand if you visualise how this material exists in its natural state.

I often think of the timber I use as a square tree, if I use it in the way it was designed to exist in nature it will usually perform better. If we alter the design of millennia then it will take more intervention and the more we intervene, the more we lose the essence of the material. Treat the wood as if it were a tree and ask yourself what the tree would want. Try to think of the frame of a building as essentially just an efficiently organised layout of tree trunks.

Understanding the properties of wood also helps us understand how it can be used in construction as a support. Wood has less strength when placed horizontally because it has a lower tensile strength, which is the resistance to forces that act across the grain. For this reason it often needs support. However, not all wood is the same. For example, oak has a much higher tensile strength than other varieties and this is why it was traditionally used to make the heavy, horizontal beams in old buildings. I remember when I was a child I would climb a nearby oak tree and run along the long, thick branches that jutted out from the trunk and made the tree almost as wide as it was tall.

The strength of wood is also determined by its 'quality'. By looking at a piece of wood you can get information about the structural composition of that wood, which will help you decide how that piece of wood should be used. One easily observable structural sign is the knot. A knot is the base of a side branch, it can often be seen as a darker, roughly circular shape around which the wood grain flows. A knot can be nice to look at and if it is on the surface of a table it can be exploited for visual effect. The layers of growth in the branches of trees, especially the lower limbs, are not so intimately joined because they are designed to die and drop off. Since knots affect cracking, warping and ease of working, they are defects that weaken timber and lower its value for structural purposes.

This weakening is far more serious when timber is subjected to forces perpendicular to the grain, so when the wood is used as a beam its strength is determined by the number and position of the knots within the wood. If you think about the compression and the tension involved in a beam, knots on the upper side are under compression so are less likely to split than knots on the lower side because these are under tension.

I built my own shed using largely recycled materials, but recycling should be understood on two levels – one of economics, one

of ethics. If you view it from only an economic perspective, the results can be disappointing. Recycled materials are often expensive because they usually need to be altered and this means paying labour time. If you are building your shed yourself, it makes all kinds of designs and materials possible. It allows you to take your time and not to be forced into decisions because of deadlines. This time becomes a part of you and your shed, and it gives you a relationship with your shed that you would never have experienced before. It allows you to slow down and to work with materials in a more meaningful way.

When I see old barns or buildings with exposed beams, I love to see the joints, the cuts, the chisel marks – I imagine the hand that crafted them and I am taken back to the time when it was built. I think of the person at work and what their life would have been like. When you work on something yourself, your spirit exists within that object because it can be perceived in a moment of time by someone else, like a ghost. Even if you cannot build your own shed, try to do something – treat it with oil, put the shelves up – it will bring you into physical contact with it. Perhaps someone will see your handiwork one day – it may not seem important but these things do matter; they give life a deeper resonance because they connect our lives with the past and the future.

ADVICE FROM AN OLD HAND

As your skills develop and you become more familiar with your tools and materials, you will begin to be more aware of good quality work. This works in two ways, you will be more attuned to poorer quality work and the feelings of being pleasantly surprised at your work are now replaced with frustration or disappointment, but being aware of these flaws is, in fact, a sign that you are progressing.

I could write a whole book on how to improve any one of the various carpentry skills needed to make a shed, but that is not the overall aim of this book. However, I have decided to include a little advice from an experienced hand about some of the useful things that you will not find in a textbook – about the realities of bringing home a good job on time and on budget.

Preparation
There are some words I would hear on site which spring to mind. Preparation and planning prevent piss poor performance (it wouldn't be right to have a book on building without at least one proper builder's

phrase). Preparation is not always essential, but it is always useful and, if you want your build to go well, there is no substitute for planning. My advice is to prepare as much as you can before the build starts, but your preparation should also continue throughout the job. By this, I mean think ahead. For example, when I am waiting for the initial materials delivery, I will have the garden ready – I will know the most efficient place to stack the wood, in what order the wood will be needed and how it will be covered that night. Another example might be checking the work schedule every night. I will consider jobs at least two days in advance so I can be sure I have the right tools and materials in place.

Tidy Up

I would suggest this is the single most neglected aspect of the novice builder. I remember when I was an apprentice if there was any downtime at all, I would be told to tidy up even if the place looked spotlessly clean. At the time, I thought it was a pointless exercise since often the next job we were doing would be a messy one, but it is not until you have experience of running a job that you understand how important it is. A tidy workplace is safer, it is more efficient and it allows you to see how well or badly a job is going. A tidy workplace is only the start, you should keep a tidy workbench so that all cuts are ready to take place immediately, you should have a tidy tool box so that you can put your hand to a tool immediately and you should have a tidy mind so you are focused on what you are doing. My advice to maximise efficiency is to get into the habit of straightening things up in the morning before you start work by preparing your tools for the day, have a tidy-up before lunch and finally before you leave at the end of the day.

Do a Job Once... Properly

Doing a job properly comes down to care. This is a simple word but it has a lot of significance to a shed builder. Care has as much to do with your state of mind as it does with your skills as a carpenter. I have learned to my expense over the years that no matter what pressure you are under, it is seldom worth rushing a job because it will ultimately cost you more time in the long run. Any mistakes you make will not only mean you have to do the job again, but unseen mistakes or having a 'that will do' attitude will have repercussions, or as I say, 'it will kick on'.

For example, if you are screwing an OSB board into a 4in x 2in upright and the screw isn't driven in properly, this could mean the board kicks

out, then the batten which goes on top of the board will kick out, which will kick out the cladding and in turn can affect the shape of the shed or potentially hamper a job such as fitting windows, and before you know it you're desperately trying to plane wood down or find some other solution to make good, when originally you could have simply taken a few seconds to re-screw. The more experience you have as a builder, the more you learn to respect this. Another example is accuracy. If I am working in millimetres I will expect to work within a 1mm tolerance, otherwise what is the point of measuring to the millimetre. It is just as easy to sharpen your pencil, to measure and mark accurately as it is to do it badly, so why not do a job well. You should condition yourself to working in the right way and it will give you the best results even if at first they may seem more difficult.

Know the Right Pace

The skill of a good chippie could be generally understood as their ability to produce quality work at a fast pace. To get to this position takes time and experience – sometimes years, sometimes a lifetime and sometimes it is the case that it will never happen and you just have to choose between the two. If you need to make the choice between quality and speed, my advice is to choose quality whenever possible as it will probably be more efficient in the long run and it will make you a happier person. It is also important to understand that different jobs have different paces and an ability to switch between paces is going to make you work better. An example might be framing out a shed which is often done at a fast pace, but within this pace there should be moments of calm and stillness while you measure and check the build.

It's All About the Flow

The flow is something that is difficult to accurately describe, but I'm going to try my best. The flow is an optimum performance level within an efficient system. It is the result of the symbiotic relationship between working well and feeling good. I actually find the creation of workflow really interesting, especially in building, it is both simple and complicated at the same time. The flow has a lot to do with having the right tools and materials to hand, but just as much to do with creating the right environment to work in both physically and mentally. Good morale is essential. Sometimes you will need to turn the music on to get things going. It also helps to acknowledge good work. A good flow can transform the enjoyment of your work day and when things are going well, it can genuinely approach being spiritual and that is the Holy Grail of Building.

Systems are There to Help You

The more jobs you do, the more you realise the importance of systems. Systems will help create a good flow. Systems often work best when there are two or more people because by compartmentalising a task into a series of stages, different people can be 'set up' to complete these specific stages without changing tools, etc. Ideally you want to get to a position whereby you are all taking on equal amounts of work towards the intended goal. Besides this being efficient, it will also give you momentum. Once you get used to being able to organise the most efficient way to do things, it will stay with you and it will get you through the hard days. As much as it is an unsavoury word, you should again 'condition' yourself to systems of good practice because these are what will help you avoid mistakes when you are tired.

Finish Each Stage

I usually split my job into logical stages. I try to never move on from any job or series of jobs until I am completely satisfied that the stage is complete to the standard I want. Not doing this can ultimately ruin the flow of not just one stage but the whole build. You need to avoid going back and forth, changing tools, setting up and packing down. This might seem obvious, but when you are tired or the pressure is on, it can be tempting to move on to the easier or more enjoyable tasks to keep your morale high or make it feel like you have had a good day's work, but this will never save you time and it is a sign that your mind is not in the right place for building. Problems and even mistakes will always occur on bespoke builds because it is impossible to predict every outcome. The trick to good building is to try and minimise problems but more importantly to confront them immediately. The longer you leave a problem the worse it will get. Even the little jobs that you do not finish can add up. You should aim to do snagging in one day – trust me a long list of snagging jobs can be demoralising.

Use Your Eyes

Get used to using your eyes, there are so many tools today giving you information about the progress of your build – levels, digital angle rules, laser-range finders – that we forget to use the most important tools of all. Measuring tapes and levels are absolutely essential, but they can miss things that the eye will not. I will walk onto a job and be able to see straightaway if the build is a good one without measuring a thing. You should get used to using your eyes to take in information about the build continuously throughout the day. Every time I walk from one corner to the next, when I change jobs or go to lunch or bend down to pick up a screw I've dropped, I will instinctively close one eye and check the horizontal and vertical parallel lines of the build. It should be standard practice to 'eye up' every length of wood before cutting, especially these days since modern fast-grown timber seems to warp with the slightest change in temperature. Your eyes are also a good indicator. I am a strong believer that we have a natural instinct for aesthetically pleasing proportions (such as the golden ratio – the aesthetically pleasing proportions that appear in geometry and patterns of nature) if you trust yourself. If a build looks right, then more often than not it will be right.

Connect Each Job

When I am training people, I try to teach them early on to be aware of the connection between the jobs. By understanding how one job links to all subsequent jobs you are much less likely to make a mistake. For example, when framing a roof out, be aware that the plywood will be sitting on this roof so try to hit the pre-cut plywood sizes, then be aware of the rubber on top of the ply and how it will go into a gutter so you can cut it the right distance from the wall and so on. It is the ability to work on a small scale while holding the entire job in your mind that separates the novice from the advanced builder. There are some builders who are among the most intelligent people I know. They may not always have the greatest language skills, but their ability to hold vast amounts of connected information in their minds is exceptional.

Fuel Up

Make no mistake, building work is a highly physical job and the potential for both physical and mental fatigue should not be underestimated. Carrying hundreds of lengths of timber through a house because there is no access or lifting 18mm ply onto a roof are jobs the office muscles will not be used to and a morning stretch may be wise especially for those of more advanced years. A structured day to keep your energy levels at a reasonably constant level is crucial, not just because of speed and flow but because of mistakes, and remember when you are constantly surrounded by power tools mistakes can have a more dramatic significance.

My daily routine consists of work from 8.30am to 5.30pm with a lunch break at 11.00am and snack break at 2.30pm. This structure has regular work intervals and therefore maximises energy levels. I will have a large bowl of porridge and a head-clearing coffee in the morning, a light lunch will not do the job, so go large. I try to mix things up and I will always try to have some form of slow-release carbohydrate, so I am not participating too often in that favourite pastime: the builder's breakfast. On my way back from the café, I will buy some fruit, nuts and a drink for the snack break. These breaks are physical breaks, but they also help to clear the mind from stress and from the long list of numbers and variables that can sometimes pile up, so try to talk about something other than the job for a bit.

Reward Yourself

In life you should work hard, really hard if you have to. It is good to be hard on yourself because this will make you progress, but there is no point to anything if you cannot reward yourself sometimes. It doesn't have to be much, maybe a beer on Fridays, maybe just a silent pat on the back from time to time. Seeing the results of your hard work and being happy about it is what separates shed building from the meaningless office job and makes it fulfilling work.

CASE STUDY

The Workshop Shed
Approximate size: 60m²

The Brief

The concept of the workshop shed was to design a place that would be able to store the necessary tools and equipment to manage the land around it, while also acting as a workshop capable of generating money if need be. The shed was built onto the existing walls of an old swimming pool and its area needed to be maximised within the constraints of permitted development, while remaining in keeping with the countryside that surrounds it.

The Design

The workshop shed was built for my cousin Robbie, who I used to build lofts with in London. It sits between his house and his farmland, on the borders of the Peak District National Park in the north of England. The shed needed to be as large as possible in order to be ultra-practical. When maximising the amount of space in a shed, often many of the design decisions are made for you. Since the shed was to be built on the old swimming pool walls, the footprint was already determined. The height of the shed was defined by the permitted development planning rules, so the only decision on the structure was the angle of the roof pitch. This decision came down to a balance between making it as shallow as possible so the soil didn't just fall off and as steep as possible so it could take the weight of all that soil. I have noticed with experienced builders that there is often a level of intuition involved, but this wasn't an easy decision as Robbie explains:

'There was going to be 180mm of soil and 10ft of snowfall is possible here, so if you add that on to the roof, there is a lot of weight involved. I tried to work it out with snow loads, but it was difficult to be sure. I came up with a number then I called my dad to ask what he would do if he was building it where he was in Canada and he came up with exactly the same figures as I did, so that was good enough for me. We designed it to take something like 500kg per metre. The other concern was the foundations, because with this amount of weight it could potentially sink, but since it was built on swimming pool foundations I knew this would be ok.'

Regarding how the shed would look from the outside, there wasn't a specific style but it needed to be in keeping with the countryside. The aim of good design in the countryside is to minimise visual impact, while maximising practical use. The blackened timber, wooden doors and stone walls all appear quiet and unassuming to the passing eye, but by far the most important part of the shed's inconspicuous aesthetic is the grass roof. Robbie was set on this feature from the beginning:

'I knew I wanted a living roof, but I didn't want a sedum roof; I wanted something you would find on the ground here and although there are no wildflower meadows in the area there would have been before it was used for sheep or farmland. I'm a big fan of the traditional Norwegian sod roof, but I've used modern materials so I don't have to redo it every 10 years or so.'

The Build

The build was started in the winter and my memories of working up in Derbyshire at this time of year involved a certain amount of coping with the weather. There was a fine mist of constant cold rain for periods while we worked, but when the sun would rise on crisp winter mornings the views across the fields were stunning. The framework went up fast, partly because Robbie and I had worked together previously for so long. There is a flow that comes with trust on site. When you have confidence that measurements are going to be right and cuts are going to be good, your mind can focus on the job at hand and it speeds the whole process up.

When framing the roof, the joists hit the 18mm ply board sizes for efficiency and immediately it felt really strong. One thing we didn't predict was that when the bitumen waterproofing went on, it became slippery especially with a fine mist of water and this made it really difficult to work on because of the pitch. The steep pitch also had consequences when it came to the grass roof. Since a heavy downfall of rain would potentially just wash all the soil away, Robbie built a lattice of non-treated mostly 2in x 2in timber in the roof, so in the future it will rot down. He couldn't screw it into the roof because it would obviously penetrate the waterproofing, so he made a cradle which sits on the ridge and hangs down. The type of plants and the conditions in which they grow also needed some thinking about:

'Once the wild flowers and grasses are established they win the battle and hold it all together, but it's getting to that point. One of the most difficult parts was sourcing the low fertility soil that is needed for the right type of growth. It was much harder than expected. I was sure I would be able to get it from around here, but in the end I had to get it delivered all the way from Liverpool. If you just put normal soil up there, the nettles and weeds start to grow and then take control.'

The Finished Shed

The first thing you notice about the shed is the harmony it has with the environment. The living roof camouflages it against a wild and rugged landscape, so much so that you don't notice the build until you are quite close to it. Robbie planted tulip bulbs in the roof, but he prefers it when the roof is in all its wild splendour:

'When people are buying eggs from the farm next door, they look over the wall and they see the flowers up in the air, and most people love it, but when the flowers die back, they don't even see it. To some people it might seem messy, but they don't necessarily understand things like, when it's all dying off, the goldfinches are in there eating the seeds.'

Over time, Robbie worked on the inside and used his years in carpentry to make a space that is efficient and flexible. Now that the shed is finished, Robbie's ideas have been put to the test. The concept of a build 'designing itself' extends to the interior of the build if you consider the most effective way to use tools and equipment. Although he considers much of the design to be common sense, I think it is a mixture of experience and intelligence:

'I knew I wanted lots of separate worktops and the most important thing was to make them all the same height so that if I wanted to build something big they would act as one surface. I built a stable in here by constructing the walls and then sliding them out through the doors. There is a bench along the whole of one side wall; any time you have a chop saw, you need to have a long area and I can easily get 6m lengths of wood in here. When you've been working for 30 years, these things are just common sense, but if I'd have built the shed when I was 15, it would have been completely different.'

The balance between using new and old materials, as well as modern and traditional methods, is something I find interesting. I meet people that are from both ends of the spectrum in terms of their outlook. Like all things it is about getting the balance right. New insulation and waterproofing materials, such as breathable membranes, are always worth using, but it's interesting to hear Robbie's perspective on power generation:

'Originally I wanted a log burner but I'm going to add an extension and have solar panels that will power a nice little electric radiator that keeps a steady temperature. It's so well insulated in here, the only thing that isn't insulated is the doors, so it won't cost much to heat it. It's more romantic to have a log burner and I would have done if I didn't have such a big burner in the house. If I had one in here, it would actually be using wood that I haven't got; the offcuts I use in my work get used up as fast as they are made. I had a plan to be quite traditional, but things change. As long as you're willing to mould yourself to the answers, you don't always have to be old-fashioned.'

You can't really have any form of heating in a build without the use of insulation because it will condense into moisture. Insulation is everything to a build like this because it gets so cold in the winter months. Insulating a building this size can be very expensive, but with walls a metre thick, a substantial grass roof and the fact there are no windows, the design has certainly helped. Robbie has also managed to get around the expense of heating by using a mixture of recycling and sensible planning:

'If you come into the workshop on a hot summer's day, it's as cool as anything. I'm trying to get as close as possible to a constant 12 degrees which is the temperature of a cave, that way it's going to be comfortable to use in any season and it will be at its most energy efficient. I'm obsessed with recycling, a lot of the Kingspan was leftovers that I would bring home from jobs and whenever we get any polystyrene packaging, that goes into the walls. I also have lots of my own sheep's wool in here, when I took it to the wool marketing board, I only got £2 for it, so I thought it's not worth it. I've only got 16 sheep, so I give some of the wool to the locals for them to spin and knit with, and I shove the rest in all the gaps in the walls. As well as the heat-loss prevention, I'm trying to get the shed as soundproof as possible so I can blast my music out when I'm working.'

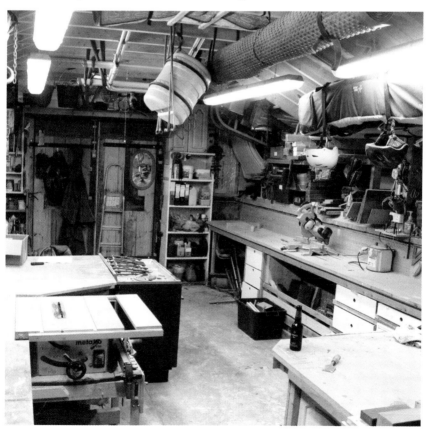

Conclusion

This shed captures the essence of what good shed design is all about, its large size is supremely functional and at the same time it effortlessly disappears into its surroundings. In a way, it is inseparable from its surroundings; the aspirations of living in the country are made possible by a structure such as this. It's difficult, if not impossible, to work in these conditions without shelter and storage. Robbie concurs:

'There is a certain amount of equipment you need to have in the country, chain saws, strimmers with all their fittings, as well as all the usual ground-working tools. You need to have somewhere out of the weather where you can quickly put your hand to something. We have horse stuff in here, I have my kayaks and my mountain bikes, my carpentry stuff and I've even decided to have a bit of an office in here. I want my house to be devoid of anything work related, so when I come out here I know this is workspace. If I go into the house to watch a film or whatever, I don't want to turn around and see paperwork or stuff to do.'

As Robbie sits in here with a beer, his family inside the house and Woody, the biggest dog I've ever met at his side, there is a quiet assurance in their air. The workshop shed is the space that Robbie has always dreamed of. As well as being an escape and a means to make money, it has given him a creative outlet. There is something else that comes with the shed: a sense of grounding. When he first moved to the countryside there was the inevitable restlessness that follows leaving a high-paced city life. Inside the structure of these walls is the framework for a new life and once he had adjusted to the stability this shed gave him, I think a certain amount of peace followed:

'A lot of stuff in here has been following me round since I was a kid. The butterfly marquetry patterns on the wall are from my cabinet-making days, all my music from over the years, my pictures and my BMX trophies are in here. If you're a tradesman you have lots of tools, but living in a tiny flat in London you never have any space. One time my room in London was just 5ft x 6ft, and I never had a vehicle, so everything I owned was in my tool box. Some of the tools I've had since I was 16, so they've followed me around for all this time. In my mind, I always had the idea that one day I would have a base for myself and all my things, and once you have a shed it becomes that place.'

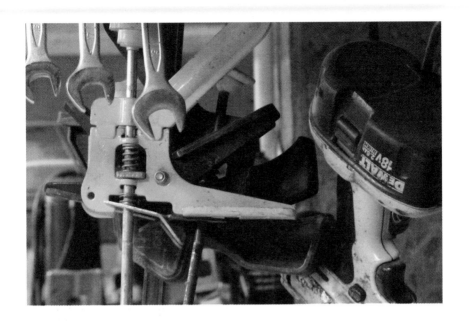

THE TOOLS

Building work is not possible without tools. The type of tools you use and the way in which you use them determines whether your build will be a good or a bad one. Knowledge is not enough, you have to take that knowledge and put it into your hands or it is useless. This takes time and experience and blisters and cuts. That is why the work is honest. You cannot pretend with words like in some professions, the proof of your skill lies in what you can do with your tools.

The respect you give to your tools says something about you as a carpenter and as a person. In the 'old days' (in which I am now including my carpentry beginnings) when a new carpenter would turn up to a job, the foreman would immediately cast a judging eye over their tool kit – this first impression was important. Next, there would follow a sort of fabricated scenario in which the foreman would say something along the lines of, 'there isn't much work this morning so why don't you knock up a couple of saw stools while you're waiting so you are ready for work.' The point being that the saw stool can be made of any old scraps of wood that are lying around the building site. There are no hard-and-fast rules to their construction, but they should be well proportioned and stable by using a 1:4 angle to splay the legs outwards. The foreman would return in half an hour, slightly sooner than had been arranged. If in that time you had made two good-looking stools with tapered legs upon which you were gently sharpening your chisels to return them to your perfectly ordered tool box, then your afternoon job had the potential to be a favourable one. If in that time you were sat on the floor with a mess of various blunt tools around your feet and one botched together rickety saw stool, your fate would be sealed. This was in essence your job interview, there was no talk of your best and worst attributes, of psychometric testing or of how you see your career in five years' time; if your work wasn't good enough, it was 'get your tools and go home' or words to that effect.

These wonderfully uncomplicated exchanges have gone now, I couldn't tell you the exact reason why, but that glance from fellow workers or employers towards your tool kit remains and for good reason. For example, I am continually perplexed to see a person pull out an old, cheap tape measure with a kink somewhere close to its most used point, and struggle with it over and over, day after day, exuding a relentless crapness. I want to say to them (and often do in fact), this job you're doing and the time that passes while you are doing it – this is your time that you waste and therefore it is your life that you waste. So, next time you're in the market for some toolage, why not get yourself something nice – get the best tool instead of the worst and then enjoy using it. Respect it and it will be good to you. That is what all this is about: respecting your tools and the time we have here on earth and expressing that respect with a love for what you do.

Hand Tools

Hand tools are the staple diet of carpentry, and there are certain hand tools I use right through the day. Lately I have been travelling between jobs more and more, so I have gradually worked on a trustworthy and efficient hand tool kit that will fit into a backpack. This portable kit, a mixture of versatile and very specific hand tools, allows me to do most shed-building jobs. Everyone has their own set of favourite tools for different reasons and there are no rules, it is all about becoming familiar with your equipment. Some carpenters seem to have a tool and a drill bit for every application known to man, and as long as they can use them properly that is great. Whereas, some of the best carpenters I have worked with have relatively few tools. For example, I love to see someone working well with a small, sharp axe.

I could easily fill a chapter on any single hand tool and its application, but for the purposes of this book, my 'essential' portable tool kit is going to work well and give you enough knowledge to adapt for your own purposes. So, here is a breakdown of the various tools I use every day and some details as to why they are so useful.

Stanley FatMax Backpack

I have had various organising systems over the years and continue to do so. Having the ability to put your hand to a tool quickly is essential to your work day. Everyone has a different method of organising, and this is fine, what is important is just that you have one. A backpack is my method because it is portable, I can put it on the back of my scooter or easily carry it on the bus or train. The Stanley FatMax backpack has a solid bottom which means its stands upright when I put it down, making finding my tools easier. It also means on wet or muddy ground everything stays clean and dry. It has good strong straps because any collection of tools is usually heavy and lots of compartments so I can separate and therefore organise tools so they are quicker to find.

DeWalt Leather Tool Belt with Brimarc Braces

I've owned this tool belt for over 12 years; it's a great example of how spending more money on something of quality can save you money. I discovered that Brimarc braces have clips wide enough to grip my thick tool belt, taking some pressure off my lower back. Because I have owned the belt for so long, my hands know exactly where everything is and the process of changing tools has the same muscle memory that exists when using the tools. What I am keen to have with a tool belt is a means to carry a tape measure, a hammer, a knife and at least one pocket in which I can easily have access to the nails or screws I am using. The belt should also preferably have a means to carry both a screw gun and a nail gun in the form of a holster or hook, so you can climb up a ladder or onto a roof with both hands free. It is also common for me to have a square and a pencil in my belt.

Tajima Pull Saw

On every job, you should buy a new sharp hand saw, there are many times when it is just not possible to use a powered saw and besides it is good practice to use a hand saw to keep your muscles and your technique up to scratch. I like this Tajima pull saw because it fits into my backpack, but also because it is nice to use once you get used to it. Pull saws make logical sense in that the act of pulling means they are cutting while under tension instead of compression thus avoiding those awkward bendy saw moments.

FatMax 450 Box Level

A level is absolutely essential to the shed build and should be used constantly throughout the day to check and re-check wall plates, window frames, uprights and basically anything around site that is still for long enough (apart from the labourer)! This level is a decent size for my backpack, I find it to be sensitive which is a good thing and I've heard they are quite robust so it should last a while.

In my tool belt, I usually carry:

Stanley FatMax 8m tape measure

Most of my builds are around 5m x 3m so an 8m tape is usually all I need. I find this one to be strong and it will extend a long way, so I can use it without help. It also seems to last a long time because the plastic coating protects it from the rain. It's useful to have both imperial and metric measurements because it is still the case that you will need to convert certain material dimensions.

Estwing Weight Forward Framing Hammer

Some might say a hammer is just a hammer, but its purpose determines the size and weight. For shed building, I happen to like this 17oz framing hammer. I am not a massive guy but I find this hammer gives me enough beef to get most jobs done. The square strike point helps to keep framing work straight, but it is unbelievably painful when you hit your fingers. So, don't!

Site Multi-Tool Knife

This knife doesn't have any special quality about it, but it is a good example of a tool that you 'just like'. The most common knife job for the shed builder is probably sharpening pencils, but without this your work becomes sloppy. It is also common to cut plasterboards or help with a neat hinge fitting. I am used to this knife, it fits nicely into my hand and my tool belt. It also has a strange mini saw which is not so useful in itself, but the saw has a flat end and the amount of times it has come in handy is ridiculous – opening tins of paint, removing an old screw when the thread has gone, that type of thing. Bespoke building is by its nature not always predictable so sometimes a tool you know and like is valuable.

Blackedge Hard Pencils

Don't forget to buy pencils. If I could have the time back that I have spent looking for pencils on site, I would... probably spend it looking for my car keys. There are, of course, lots of pencils on the market. I like these Blackedge ones because they seem to last longer, especially the hard ones; square carpenter's pencils do not roll away should you need to be on a roof and supposedly they don't follow the grain of the wood when marking out lines. I also think it is just good to use a carpenter's pencil, they feel right in the hand and I actually find them versatile for sketching because they act like an italic pen making both a thick and thin line possible. The drawings in this book were done using a carpenter's pencil.

Nail Punch

Often overlooked and somewhat underrated, if you need to sink a nail beneath the surface of the wood, this cheap tool is the one that will do it without damaging the wood around it. So, get one.

In my tool bag, you would find:

Stanley FatMax Foldaway Chisel

The condition of your chisels tells a story about what kind of workman you are, so try to find some time to keep them sharp. On specific work days, I will bring my chisel roll and sharpening stone, but this foldaway chisel is handy to transport and fits into my tool belt nicely. Chisels are important for hanging doors, but useful to have on you for awkward bits of wood that need to be removed or altered. This one has a good metal strike point, which some of the other foldaway ones don't.

FatMax Compact Chalk Line

Since my backpack will not carry a 2.4m aluminium straight edge, the old faithful chalk line is still the best way to get a straight line of any distance. They will all do a job; I would only say perhaps choose one that is easy to refill and has a retractable geared string to save you winding time.

Flathead Screwdriver

The flathead has become rarer in the power tool age because flathead bits for your screw gun are just not meant to be. But it is nice to use certain finishing screws and leave them parallel with the floor so they look neater. I personally always have a couple of flathead screwdrivers, because I frequently have to remove the old rusted hinges from a second-hand

door, and with a traditional screwdriver it is easier to apply the downward pressure needed. A flathead is also going to be useful when the fuse goes in your extension lead, disabling every power tool you own!

Fisco Plastic Roofer's Square

A square will be used throughout the day, it's essential for a quick, square pencil mark or cut and especially useful when making accurate square cuts using a circular saw. I bought this plastic square because whenever possible it's good to try to keep the weight of my backpack down. This might sound a bit mad when you look at my hammer but, like I said, whenever possible.

Sliding Bevel

The sliding bevel is just a simple and marvellous tool that is difficult to improve. In my carpentry life, I have used it mostly for finding the angle of a roof, then transposing this angle to the skill saw or chop saw for angled cuts, but there are other times in shed building when an angle size is needed. It is useful to mark any angles on your bench and label them, so they can be checked from time to time should the bevel get dropped.

Roughneck Ratchet Clamp

I often use clamps to help give me a rough framework on a shed at the very beginning of a job. I also use them to help me work alone or when I don't want to disturb others from what they're doing, and I need help to keep a piece of wood still or to hold two pieces of wood together when cutting. These clamps are really quick to secure or release and different sized ones can be used for any fixing purpose such as gluing together doors or workbenches.

In my drill rolls are:

Trend Snappy Countersinks
I use these for lots of things, mostly for window and door frames. They help to avoid splitting wood by drilling a pilot hole, and sink the screw beneath the surface so it can be covered up.

Armeg Beaver Drill Bits
These are great for getting through wood fast. They are similar to auger bits, which remove the wood as you drill so it doesn't clog things up. I have a long one to get through double joists and a stubby one for when there is not much room between joists for my screw gun.

Spare Bit Holders
These are important should you drop one into the next-door neighbours' nettle patch, which is more often than you might think. It is also good to have some good quality masonry bits to help with getting into concrete or brickwork when the need arises, but remember to choose the sizes that are compatible with plug sizes.

Wera Drill Bits and Magnetic Holder
I find these hard wearing. If the labourer has a poor technique I give him my slightly cheaper (but still good) DeWalt bits. The magnetic holder with these Wera bits is very useful. Sometimes with shed building you can find yourself in precarious positions and are able only to screw one-handed. In this scenario the magnetic holder will save you a lot of time.

My personal kit includes:

Folding Ear Protectors
If you want to save your hearing, and trust me you do, then use some form of ear protection. It's not only going to be your ears you're saving, but your sanity when you get that high-pitched ringing noise from using a circular

saw all day in an enclosed room. The other option is buying moulded noise-cancelling protectors. These can be expensive but are worth it in the long run. I like these folding protectors because small things, such as packing tools away easily when you are tired, can make a real difference to your day.

Kevlar Gloves

I have used all kinds of different gloves for winter work and these are great for cold days. Most woolly gloves will last around 5–6 minutes on a job, but these genuinely and rather unbelievably can last me all year!

Petzel Head Torch

Petzel make good quality, waterproof head torches. Head torches keep your hands free and allow you to see in dark places, need I say more?

Snood

A snood is great for the cold. I find as long as I don't have a draft down my neck or my waist then I can work in pretty cold conditions. I also use it as a face mask to help stop breathing in sawdust. A proper mask is a better idea, but they can be uncomfortable to wear all day and the reality is they get thrown away. A snood may not be the best filter, but it's better than using nothing!

Travel First Aid Kit and Painkillers

The most frequently used first aid device in my carpentry career has been masking tape, used to try and stick together a nasty gash so you can keep working or drive to hospital. But it's a good idea to have a first aid kit with antiseptic wipes, gauze and sterile tape to give you the best chance of healing quicker.

It may be some time before you are happy with the set of hand tools you put together. You may want to go out and buy a large selection of brand new tools, you may want to gradually piece your kit together over time. A tool kit is something that continues to change and grow in your life. I still love to trawl through car boot sales in search of an ugly hand-crafted nineteenth-century hammer or beautiful-looking 4in chisel that just needs a sharpen to bring it back to life. Whatever hand tools you choose or however you obtain them, the important thing is that you use them over and over again until you are familiar with them. Master the movements involved so they become instinctive, understand how much pressure to use, how much strength is required, the position of your tool and the position of your hands. In any walk of life, there is nothing quite like seeing a person who uses a given tool with such sensitivity and accuracy that it becomes an extension of the hand itself. When you grow more confident with your hand tools, you will become calmer and you will work better, and importantly you will enjoy the time you spend working more.

Power Tools

In essence, power tools are machines to save you time and effort. In the right hands, they can transform a job by expanding the possibilities of design and construction, increasing complexity and decreasing cost. In the wrong hands, they can ruin expensive materials and remove useful body parts.

Power is not always a necessity. These days it is easy to become a little too reliant on power tools (and I include myself in this). Modern power tools are very impressive and we can all get seduced by new models with increased torque and longer battery life. Power tools can certainly help you to achieve a fast result, but bear in mind that it is not always a new power tool you should be reaching for; sometimes it is a new skill you need to be learning. Power tools should be an addition to your hand tool kit, not a replacement for it.

There are low-cost gems that pop into power tool circles from time to time, but these are few and far between. The majority of time you are getting what you pay for and the difference between good and bad power tools is usually greater than the difference between good and bad hand tools. By this, I do not mean that good hand tools aren't worth their weight in gold, because they are, it is more that a cheap power tool will often not have much power and cannot necessarily be understood as a tool! A cheap hammer will eventually make a nail go into wood, whereas I have used cheap power tools that have come straight out of the box and died within minutes of putting them to work.

Top-end brands such as Fez tools, and Mafell are going to give you the best chance of doing a great job, but they really come into their own for specialist purposes. For most shed-building jobs, mid- to high-range products such as DeWalt, Makita, Bosch and Hitachi are going to give you the same results – these companies have a good record of churning out good quality and robust tools.

There is a certain bravado that seems to hang around power tool circles, which I am aware of but not especially keen on. For the most part it makes some sense; if you turn up to a work site with expensive tools, the probability increases that you have some kind of quality to your work, firstly because better tools can give better results, but also because you have had to buy the expensive tools, which suggests a certain level of success.

But I have learned from experience that the lack of skill some workers have knows no bounds, and it is remarkable to see at first hand the mess a good tool in the wrong hands can make of a job.

There are the purists among us who prefer to use only hand tools in carpentry. I am absolutely respectful of this and I understand that when motivated to recreate a particular period or genre of carpentry then the tools relevant to this time will give an appreciation of what those guys went through. It is also worth remembering that power tools are great! There are some parts of life that progress for a reason and this doesn't necessarily take away authenticity, it simply makes life easier.

For the same reasons as the hand tools section, I am going to strip down my kit to the essential shed-building power tools which I use almost every day.

Drill Driver

I currently use a DeWalt DCD790 brushless drill driver or screw gun. The modern drills are exceptional tools. Technology changes fast, so this model, like all models, will become dated, but the principles for choosing a new model will be the same. The brushless technology boasts longer battery life and since if a screw gun failed it was usually a problem with the brushes, this no doubt makes them more durable also. Always make sure you purchase two batteries so one is always ready to go. I chose the 2.0amp batteries instead of the 4.0amp because these give the optimum balance. Don't underestimate how a balanced tool can help you, especially at the end of a long day's work. I have always bought DeWalt drill drivers because, besides the fact they are great tools, they feel good in the hand. This screw gun will be able to do every job on the shed build that the more expensive models can. It has more than enough power for the screws I use; I specifically chose the model which had no hammer because it was a little shorter and lighter, and since I don't often need a hammer drill on a shed build, the smaller dimensions are of more value to me. It is also the little things, such as a conveniently placed

magnetic bit holder for switching from PH bits to PZ and an LED light when you press the trigger, that make the difference. Whatever model you choose, I would recommend a two-speed transmission, torque control and what they call 'an intelligent trigger' which just means the pressure applied controls the speed.

Impact Driver

The impact driver seems to have become more and more popular, perhaps because they are more powerful now and perhaps because they are often sold as a package with the drill driver. The main advantage of the impact driver is a compact design and light weight with no loss of power and a quick-change hex driver with no chuck. The impact driver is specifically engineered to do one job: drive screws. They usually and, perhaps surprisingly, deliver more turning force than a drill driver because the concussive action transfers much of the high-energy torque directly to the screw and not your wrist or forearm. In my portable kit, I actually take only the drill driver because I want the option of having a chuck so I can use a masonry drill bit if I need to. However, the gap seems to be closing with the drill driver since mini chuck and other hole-drilling accessories are becoming available.

Circular Saw

The circular saw is another workhorse on site. It is so versatile that having this saw alone is enough to build a shed. I use the Makita 190mm mains-powered circular saw. The 190mm blade will easily cut through 4in x 2in. I will also use the circular saw for cutting sheet material such as OSB and plywood to size, or for the more detailed cuts on cladding. I find this Makita saw solid and robust without being too large or cumbersome, and each time I have bought one they have lasted me for years. Whichever circular saw you choose, this is one tool I definitely would not buy cheaply. It is one of the more dangerous tools because it is used in a mobile way, so you want the balance and security the extra quality will give you. Cheaper models often burn out when you ask them to rip down a length of 4in x 2in. it is also the little things that help, such as having an accurate guide mark or hex key storage (to change the blade) in the handle for safe keeping and a metal single-action lever for quick adjustment of cutting depth, which when used properly should be set for every cut. The trick with a circular saw is to use it with a sharp blade to take the pressure off its motor and to reduce the probability of kickbacks. You should keep the saw well maintained. You often see a safety guard that sticks because it is bent on site and when it is placed on the floor still moving it crawls across the ground like an angry rodent in search of some toes to chop off, so beware!

Chop Saw

The chop saw or, to be more accurate, the sliding mitre saw will be used constantly through the job because of its speed and accuracy. All the 4in x 2in lengths that make up the framework of a build will usually be cut using the chop saw. It will also be used for cutting the batten and the external cladding to length. I have a DeWalt Mitre Saw, but I actually often use an Evolution Rage3 Sliding Mitre Saw. I wanted to put at least one cheaper model in somewhere and of all the tools I use, this is the one where a less expensive model has worked reasonably well, perhaps because it is fixed so it doesn't lose accuracy. It is sensible to screw down your chop saw and make sure it is stable. It is also worth buying the rollers, which can be placed either end of your bench to support the long lengths of wood so you don't need to have help. Again, the chop saw is dangerous and you need to focus; avoid the common but monumental error of chopping off the end of your thumb on the hand that holds the wood as you look at the pencil mark you have just made!

Framing Nail Gun

The nail gun is a simply wonderful and justifiably expensive piece of kit. Just like the powered saws, they are not strictly essential but if you are a shed builder, the amount of time it saves you on a build means it immediately pays for itself. I use the Paslode IM350. As with all power tools the technology moves fast. However, Paslode framing guns were so good in the first place that newer models are very similar with only slight design changes and longer battery life. The framing gun is a powerful tool and every person should have the chance to fire one at least once in their life. Paslode guns are powered by disposable gas and a battery to create the spark. They are heavy duty, mobile tools, but be sure not to run out of gas. The other options in the framing gun range are the battery-powered gun and the pneumatic gun. The battery-powered gun seems to be constantly evolving so expect a bigger slice of the market for these. Right now they are quieter with slightly less power. The pneumatic gun is generally less expensive but since you have to buy a compressor the overall cost evens out (although the compressor is a useful tool in itself). When it comes to safety, the nail gun is basically a gun, so this should be enough information to respect it. A common error on site is to engage the gun and fire it down the side of the timber. Another common one is to fire into a knot of wood and the nail will hit the knot and shoot sideways into your hand if it is too close.

Brad Nailer or Finishing Gun

Pin guns as I call them are used for second fixing. They are useful to the shed builder because of their speed at fixing cladding in place, but they are also used for fixing skirting boards, window frames, architrave, trim or plywood internal cladding. These pins were traditionally difficult to hammer in because of their size. I use a Paslode IM50 (which is also gas powered); the batteries are compatible with my framing gun and it is of a similar good quality. The IM50 fires f18 gauge brads, the similar Paslode IM65 fires f16 gauge brads. I generally prefer the f18 gauge because they are smaller and they disappear more easily, but the brads seem to be less available to buy; the f16 gauge still disappear and they will handle larger pieces of wood. Again, although expensive they are a wonderful tool to use and they pay for themselves in saved labour in no time at all, and also expect the battery-powered models to be more popular in the future.

Plane

The plane is useful in shed building for door hanging, cleaning up cladding, making tables or workbenches or reshaping awkward raised bits of wood. It is not essential to have one, but since purchasing one I immediately regretted not having one sooner. I have recently replaced my mains-powered plane with a DeWalt 18V Li-ion XR battery-powered plane. Battery-powered tools are becoming more and more significant with longer battery life and more power, especially since the advent of brushless technology. This model is compact and well balanced, and has a relatively long foot which makes it stable. The reason I bought this model is because firstly I trust DeWalt, but also because I am buying into their battery system. It is worth doing some research when buying battery-powered tools, not only on the tool you are buying but also on their whole battery-powered product range. You never know what tools you may want in the future and it is never ideal having to carry around a host of different chargers and batteries with different voltage and sizes when you are trying to build an efficient kit.

Palm Router

I don't often use a router, it wasn't something I ever thought I would regularly carry around with me on shed builds, but the palm router has changed this. It is an incredibly versatile, lightweight and compact piece of kit, perfect for edge moulding and fitting door furniture or finer detailing such as curved door openings on cladding, although I mostly use my router for recessing hinges. I own the Bosche 600 ¼in palm router. It is much easier to control, and far less like holding onto a Chinook than my massive ½in router. It has a nice soft start and fine height adjustment. You can buy the plunger fitting and various guides and guards, but I basically use my router freehand. These types of tools may not be used every day but the very act of building in a bespoke manner means that there is always something unpredictable that pops up on a job and if you have versatile tools, you will always be able to think of a way to solve matters.

These are the tools I consider to be the most effective when shed building but, just as with the hand tools, there are no rules and it is for you to work on a kit that can achieve the results you want. Of the other power tools on the market, you could consider: a plunge saw on tracks for accurate sheet cutting; an orbital sander for smooth finishes; angle grinders for cutting roof tiles or metal; table saws for making your own cladding; biscuit jointers for making your own desk or storage boxes, and the list goes on.

Part of the process of buying power tools is to not walk into your local store and buy on a whim; good power tools are expensive, so do your research, the tool catalogue is the shed builder's glossy mag. Trawl through the torque settings, the power ratios, the noise reduction, the good and bad reviews, and carefully consider which tools you need for the job at hand and beyond. If you can, find a shop with the model you want and hold it, check its balance and how it feels in your own hand. Remember to enjoy these moments. If you are like me, you don't often get to spend money on exactly what you want. Cherish power tool research because a good quality machine is a wonderful thing.

A note on safety, because power tools can be dangerous. Don't use faulty or damaged power tools; saving on a new purchase is never going to be worth an injury. Always work in a tidy environment and try not to borrow old tools because knowing the quirks of your own tool is being able to predict its actions. Certainly, tool quality, maintenance and technique are factors in working safely, but by far the most important aspect is in your mind. From day one, I tell people who work with me to hold the tool properly and in a well-balanced way, I try to put good practice into their bodies, I teach them the safety measures for a particular tool such as tucking in your thumb when using the chop saw, but most importantly I tell them every time you make a cut, you pause for a split second and focus only on the power tool and its action. This may not sound important but this focus and awareness is crucial.

Most injuries I have seen on site are from people who have used power tools their whole life and they become complacent. This idea of conditioning, of putting good practice into your body and your mind, is a means to fall back on good habits when you are rushing or when you are tired and the mind is wandering at the end of the day. But this doesn't mean you should be in fear of the power tool, it is an understanding of its danger and an adjustment of your behaviour that will make it safer to use. Respect your tools and give yourself a chance to have a long and healthy relationship with them, and they will be good to you and make your life easier.

PART 4

THE
BUILD

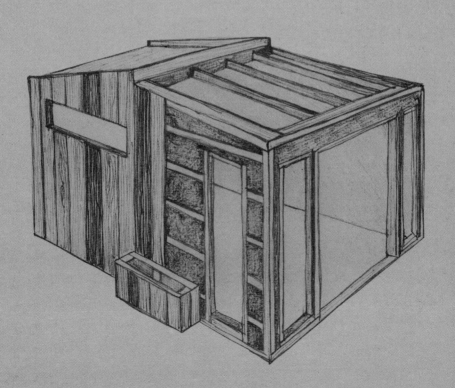

'Whatever is worth doing at all is worth doing well.'

Phillip Stanhope

SHED POSITION AND SITE PREPARATION

The ideas we have in life are so often put on the back-burner while the everyday tasks that allow us to tread water take place. Taking the kids to school, picking up bread on the way home, sorting through recent utility bills, determining whether you are allowed by the local tip to dump an old armchair and so on. But today is going to different, that eternal list of menial jobs is going to have to wait and the reason is shed. Presuming you have your shed design and rough dimensions, all the necessary planning permits and you have tactfully mentioned the build to the least favourite of your neighbours, then it is now time to set sail on the journey to make this harboured shed dream of yours a reality.

The first thing to consider as you walk into your garden, coffee in hand to survey the area, is the position of your shed. Most of the time, this will be quite self-explanatory – you will instinctively have an idea about where is the best place to put the shed and the longer you have had your garden, the more you will understand the positives and negatives of the various spaces and how they change with the seasons, but it is still beneficial to work through a series of logical steps.

The most important factors in determining the position of your shed are the orientation and topography of your house and garden, the path of the sun, the effect of trees and neighbouring walls, and the shed's size and primary function.

The orientation of your garden will define your access to daylight. It is useful to map the path of the sun to understand the light and possibly change either the shed position or the design accordingly. You may want as much natural light as possible or if you are in a warmer climate than the UK, the shade may be of more value. Let us presume for a moment that light is important to you. Try to position the larger windows so they are south facing and remember to consider the angle changes that the sun will undergo due to seasonal variations. Artists' studios will often have as much natural light as possible but the windows will be north facing to avoid direct light and shadows.

The topographical elements of relief or gradients and surrounding trees and walls, etc. can also affect your shed position. It is important to check your ground by digging an exploratory hole. This will give you information about the type of soil or other substrate you are going to be working with. Building at the bottom of a garden in a wet climate can potentially cause problems; if there is poor drainage your shed can sometimes be sitting in water, especially in the winter months. Wood and water generally do not go well together – excess water or damp can rot wood, ruin paint work, cause hinges to rust or allow mould to take hold. The combination can also make the act of building more difficult and compromise the use of the shed with muddy or waterlogged access.

Trees can also impact on the ideal position of your shed. The first concern is the size of the tree; a large tree can block out a substantial amount of light and a larger tree usually means larger roots. There are few things more back-breaking than the removal of tree roots, and when you consider the job they are designed to do, it is little wonder. They are nature's foundations and one cannot help but respect them,

although as you hack away respect may not be the emotion that is most present in your mind. It may be the case that you need to get in a specialist tree surgeon to either trim a tree or completely remove it.

If the tree is small, it may be possible to work around the roots, but keep in mind that both the tree and the roots will continue to grow and this could cause problems in the future.

You should also consider the type of tree you have. For example, deciduous trees that shed their leaves in the autumn can be more disruptive than you might imagine. I often work in London and the impressive London Plane trees that are so prevalent in the city have an equally impressive autumnal cast-off. Inevitably large trees mean regular clearing of skylights and guttering. You should also expect another cast-off from local animals that live in an overhanging tree; wood pigeons and grey squirrels are the usual suspects in Britain. Evergreens are often a little more shed-friendly, but not always – pine needles can be particularly obstructive to gutters and drainage systems, and seem to effortlessly get into every nook and cranny.

Importantly, consider your access. For example, if the shed is a metal workshop it is going to involve bringing raw materials into the build on regular occasions and therefore should be situated if possible with the best access to your local street.

I might add at this point, whatever the problems are with your shed position – whether hills, trees or access – I would try to find solutions to the problems rather than move the shed if the preferred location has clear benefits. Try to balance the pros and cons and remain positive; remember what really matters – it may be possible to add a pathway to use a trolley to transport materials, but it will never be possible to change the path of the sun. If I liked the position, then I would personally prefer to add extra hardcore for drainage or climb up onto the roof to remove leaves etc, but consider how likely or easy these things are going to be for you in the long term.

Once you have an idea of the position of your shed, it is time to make measurements and mark out the footprint to check if your drawings fit with the reality of the garden space. You could use line-marker spray for speed; I use stakes and a string line so I can change the shape and position easily. At this point, you should also measure the height so you can imagine how the build will impact your garden space and the light in your garden.

It might seem obvious, but don't be afraid to change things. My advice is to trust your judgement, if you feel the build is going to be too big or too small, or the windows are in the wrong position to catch the late afternoon sun, then adjust. You may have put a lot of time into making the size perfectly efficient to build or you may have spent hours on drawings and plans ready to send to glass suppliers, but if the build isn't right for your garden, it just isn't right. A change now won't cost anything and you will not have to live with the mistake for the rest of the shed's life.

One word of warning: don't be too cautious when it comes to the size and the impact it will have on your garden. For example, be aware that although 2.5m might seem high, a good chunk of this will be taken up with floor joists and roof joists, and the higher the finished internal roof, the more enjoyable it will be to be in. I say this from experience, I have noticed some of my clients are nervous about changing their gardens or worried about what the neighbours will think, but you have to remember that a well-designed shed can make your garden a more beautiful place and enhance the aspects that are already there.

Be confident – you know what you want and when it feels right, so trust your judgement. If you have the time, then perhaps come back to it over a couple of days to see what the area is like in the morning and in the evening. Once you are happy, my advice is to get an early night and rest, especially if you are self-building, because if there is one day that requires the muscle and sweat of honest labour it is foundation day.

FOUNDATIONS

Now that your ground is level and the position and size of your shed is set, from this point on you will be building, which means doing things right. Foundations are probably the single most neglected part of the shed build and yet are possibly the most important. If your foundations are not good, then every process after this point will become more difficult. Do not be tempted to cut corners; a good strong and level base can set up the whole build, so take some time to get it right because once the walls go up there is nothing you can do to change the foundations other than rip the shed down and start again.

The foundations need to be suitable for the size and weight of the building and they need to be achievable in line with your budget, available skills and accessibility. The most popular types of foundations to choose from are: a concrete base, a suspended wooden floor on posts, plastic flooring kits, and gravel or flagstones – all of which have their pros and cons. It may be fine for a lightweight shed to be built onto flagstones, but these are not good enough for the builds I do. So, I am going to concentrate on the concrete base and the suspended wooden floor, as in the bespoke shed build they usually give me the best results in terms of cost, strength and compatibility.

The Concrete Base or Slab

The use of a concrete base is the most expensive of the foundations and needs to be carefully considered, for while it is very good, it is also very permanent or can only be removed with a lot of hard labour. The method I use to lay a concrete foundation is a minimum two-person job and requires specific skills to achieve a professional result.

First, prepare the ground by marking out the dimensions and position of the shed using string lines. The overall height of the building should be considered in relation to planning permission and aesthetic appearance. I will often try to make foundations as close to the finished ground level as possible because ultimately this will give you more headroom. It is also worth considering the amount of earth removal that will take place, as this may require a skip.

Usually, the overall depth of a concrete base will be approximately 300mm, assuming the base is to be insulated. This consists of 100mm base preparation in the way of hardcore, 100mm for insulation and a minimum of 100mm for the concrete. Once you've prepared the ground and dug out to the required level, you need to make a shuttering frame. For this wooden planks are used, ideally 6in x 1in but as this framework is temporary, any used planks of sufficient strength timber will be fine.

Next, hammer stakes into the ground at each external corner of the string line, then further stakes at intervals to give enough strength to the framework; a good rule of thumb is usually about 1.5m apart. Then, screw the planks to the inside of the stakes at the required height; make sure they are level on the top surface as this is what you will be working to for the finished base. This framework will be the footprint of your build. You should never oversize the base as this can collect water and rainfall, which will seep under the finished shed.

If the corners of the build are to be square, then now is the time to check them. You can use a builder's square or, for a more accurate method, use that builder's favourite – the 3, 4, 5 formula otherwise known as Pythagoras's theorem. To enact the theory, simply measure down one edge to a measurement of 3, then measure down the right-angled edge to a measurement of 4 – if the right angle is perfectly square, the joining diagonal measurement between 3 and 4 will always be 5. It doesn't matter whether the measurement is millimetres, metres or miles, providing the rule of 3, 4, 5 is accurately used, the result will always be the same.

Having removed all the vegetation and large rocks, the base is now ready to build. The first step is to lay a sub-base of approximately 75–100mm of hardcore, packed down tight into a good compact surface. For the sub-base, you should use old broken bricks or buy a dedicated crushed stone.

For insulation under a concrete base, the best method is to use rigid insulation sheets which are made by many different manufacturers. These boards usually come in 8in x 4in sheets of varying thickness and can be purchased at any good builders merchant. They are easily cut to size using an old woodworking saw. Ideally for decent under floor insulation, a thickness of 100mm should be used. The price does not vary a great deal between the different thicknesses so it is hardly worth cutting corners to save money. The sheets should be laid down after the hardcore, but before the damp-proof membrane and should cover the whole floor area with no gaps.

You can now lay the damp-proof membrane (DPM), covering the whole floor area with an allowance to come up the sides of the poured concrete. In effect, a plastic bowl is being created in which to pour the concrete that will help safeguard against rising damp. If there are to be any joins in the membrane because of the floor size, then it's wise to make a good overlap and tape the joint together.

With the preparation now complete, it is time for the concrete base and the first decision to make is whether to mix on site or have a ready mix delivered. Ready mix is preferable as it is much less labour intensive. It is a constant mix compared to lots of hand mixed smaller amounts and, in any event, it usually works out less expensive than mixing by hand. Assuming access isn't a problem, it is always worth checking if any local concrete suppliers deliver and mix on site. In most areas now, suppliers will arrive with a dedicated smaller vehicle with facilities to mix on the wagon. These firms supply experienced labour and you are only paying for the amount of concrete used. A common mistake with pre-mixed concrete is ordering too much or too little. Too much and you end up scrambling around looking for places to get rid of excess or building steps you don't need. Too little and you are mixing to cover the shortfall in a rush before the first mix sets.

A basic guide for ordering the correct amount of concrete is to work out the square meterage and the depth of concrete required, then multiply the square area by the depth. For example, if the area equals 15m^2 and the depth is 0.1m, then the volume required is 1.5m^3. If ordering a ready mix, allow 10% for spillage.

If you are self-laying, the concrete needs to be poured in manageable amounts, ideally have three people to hand so one can spread concrete using a garden rake while the other two work either side of the frame, tamping the finished base level.

If the concrete is to be mixed by hand or using a cement mixer, then the mix should be a mix of 3, 2, 1. This is three parts stone chippings

preferably ¾in clean stone to two parts sharp sand to one part cement. The mix is most effective when quite wet as it will be easier to use and to make level. This will not affect the strength of the concrete. When the base is complete it should be floated off on the surface using a steel float – the better the finish, the better the floor will be when dry. It may sound obvious but the smallest lumps and blemishes can be quite severe and harsh when the concrete hardens. For this reason it is worth floating several times during the various stages of drying.

Suspended Wooden Floor

A suspended wooden floor sitting on foundation posts is my usual method of choice for shed foundations. It is the easiest, the cheapest and the most convenient method of foundation that is still capable of supporting a substantial bespoke shed. Also, because I am often carrying all the materials through a house with very little access to the site, it is sometimes the only choice I have.

Only pressure-treated timber should be used for posts and these days it is quite common to use treated wood throughout. I will usually use it for the whole of the suspended wooden floor. You may think wood protection is a relatively recent phenomenon, but the use of a treatment to extend the life of wood can be traced as far back as the Ancient Greeks. Indeed, records show that wood used for bridge building from the time of Alexander the Great was soaked in olive oil. The Romans protected their ship hulls by brushing on tar and during the Industrial Revolution wood preserving was fundamental to the progressive wood-processing industry. The market for commercial pressure treatments grew rapidly in the latter part of the nineteenth century with the growth of railways as the sleepers were then soaked in Creosote.

However, nowadays people are much more concerned over the toxicity of such treatments and the treatment process has become very effective with less personal exposure. While present-day wood preservative and pressure treatments are generally considered safe to handle, when cutting treated wood and using power tools where a lot of fine particle dust is produced it is always advisable to wear a mask.

The first job in laying your suspended floor is to mark out the floor area using string lines. I then use a landscape marking spray so I can remove the string, which makes digging the holes easier. The holes should measure approximately 300mm x 300mm by about 600mm deep, or down to firm, solid ground. A concrete pad stone is placed at the bottom of each hole or alternatively you can mix a small amount of concrete and make pad stones for the base, but this means waiting for it to set. The 4in x 4in pressure-treated posts are then cut to the required height which will be just below the finished floor level. The posts are fixed into place with dedicated quick-drying, post-fixing cement and you should expect to use a minimum of one bag per hole. An ordinary self-mixed concrete mix will do the job just as well but the saving in cost needs to be balanced against the loss of time. Dedicated pre-mix solution will set and be finished in about 20 minutes, whereas a self-mix concrete may take 24 hours. Assuming the suspended timber floor frame will be made from 5in x 2in softwood graded C16 then extra posts should be added at intervals of no more than 3m depending on the overall floor size, shape and design.

As the ground will soon be inaccessible, at this point it is a good idea to cover the footprint of the finished shed with a weed-control fabric, which will stop any unwanted growth beneath the shed while still allowing for water drainage. This material is inexpensive and is usually sold in 1m rolls that can be laid in minutes. Simply cut the material to the required lengths, overlap any joins, pin down the edges and cover with a light spreading of gravel, sand or mulch. If the base is in contact with the ground, then I will put down a layer of DPM again covering the whole footprint of the shed to stop rising damp.

For floor framing timber, I'll often use 5in x 2in because this is sufficient at 3m spans to cover most uses. However, the size of these joists should be adjusted depending on the size of the shed – there are guides at the back of the book to help. When the posts are all in place and the concrete is dry, clamp a horizontal floor frame to the posts at the correct height, make sure they are level and the posts can now be marked for cutting.

Once the cuts are made, you can fix the floor frame to the posts using galvanised or copper screws or bolts. Ideally the floor frame will sit on top of the posts and be secured with metal straps to the side. As modern treated wood has a large copper content, it is always advisable to use fixings recommended for use with treated wood because copper is particularly corrosive to ordinary steel.

Now it is time to lay the floor joists. These can either sit on joist hangers if the height is a problem or simply sit perpendicular on top of the supporting frame. All floor joists should be set at 400mm centres, depending on the span, and between the joists you should add noggins to further strengthen the base.

Before laying a finished floor surface you will need to insulate against rising cold air. The worst enemy of wood is moisture, so insulation should allow ventilation. Wood will comfortably deal with warmth or cold but where the two meet there is a tendency for condensation. Good ventilation will prevent this. You can either use chicken wire to support mineral wool insulation or you can use batten to support board insulation, either way, be sure the insulation fits nice and snug. In the case of board insulation you can use foil tape to prevent any draughts.

Once the foundations and floor frame are complete, you are ready for flooring. The ideal choice here is flooring-grade tongue-and-groove chipboard panels, which can readily be purchased at a general size of 2,400mm x 600mm x 19mm (22mm is also available). These panels should be laid at right angles to the floor joists and screwed securely in place. The tongue-and-groove joints are also glued and the whole floor acts as one unit, which increases its strength. The result is a perfectly flat strong floor, ready for any chosen finish. The floor is now finished but as it will more than likely be exposed to wet weather conditions while the rest of the build takes place, you should consider covering it with a temporary waterproof membrane that will protect the finished floor until the build is watertight.

WALL STRUCTURE AND FRAMEWORK

Putting in the framework is one of my favourite parts of the build – it's great to be out of the dirt and damp of the ground and it's a relief to spend the day in a more upright position. You can set up the power tools, load up your tool belt and, all being well, you will start to see your dreams of a shed come to life in a physical form.

Walls are multifunctional in that as well as giving the shed its shape, they are also expected to carry the weight of the roof. Wall structure and framework should be undertaken in a practical order. It is quite common in city properties with limited garden space to maximise the size of the shed by building close to a pre-existing boundary wall or walls. In such cases, I will build the walls that will sit nearest to the boundary first and complete them in their entirety on the floor before lifting them upright into place.

The framework is best built in 4in x 2in softwood pine. When buying the wood for the framework, it is always best to select wood carefully, paying attention to warped or twisted long lengths; this is not always possible

when you are getting a large delivery, but you can sometimes pay extra for better quality wood. Always try to buy in the most economical lengths for the specific build. For example, long lengths may be cheaper per metre than short lengths, but if the build requires lots of cuts at 2.1m, then it may be uneconomical to buy 6m lengths with 1.8m off-cuts when 4.2m lengths are available.

Ideally, the back wall should be built first and to keep things simple, I will assume there are no doors and windows at this point. The framework begins with a horizontal top and bottom plate – 100mm being the width, 50mm being the height. Then the uprights are cut at the required height and fixed between the plates with a nail gun if available. It is usual to start with the corners and then space the other uprights at intervals best suited to the wooden panel boards that will be used to brace the structure. Panel boards are usually supplied in 1,220mm width by 2,440mm length, so structural centres would in this case be 610mm, but you can adjust to suit with this being a maximum measurement. Next, fix noggins or cross members in the vertical gaps, depending on the size of the structure. I will often fix these at the same height as plasterboard sizes, which are multiples of either 900mm or 1,200mm. These noggins give the structure extra strength and help with any sideways movement.

Then, the whole exterior face needs to be boarded out with 11mm OSB (sterling board) and fixed to the framework with the appropriate screws. OSB is relatively inexpensive and is adequate for giving the framework structure and a good lateral strength. Now, cover the whole surface with a breathable membrane, which should be fixed directly to the OSB with a staple gun and overlap any joints by 100mm. The breathable membrane is an important stage and is often ignored to save expense. However, the benefits outweigh the costs. Breathable membrane is waterproof yet extremely permeable to water vapour, allowing the structure to breathe and protecting it from condensation. The shed can also potentially be left in this state for a while, remaining protected until it is clad.

The next job is to fix 2in x 1in batten along the full width or height of the structure. Roof batten are ideal for this purpose as they are inexpensive and plentiful. Whether these batten are fixed horizontally or vertically is dependent on the chosen finished cladding. If it is a vertical cladding, then the batten will be fixed horizontally, likewise if it is horizontal cladding then the batten will be fixed vertically. In any event, the batten should be securely fixed straight through to the main frame using appropriate length screws or nails. The cladding is now fitted directly to the batten according to the type of cladding chosen, which will be explained in more detail later.

The wall structure is now complete and ready for permanent placement. Depending on the size of this wall, some extra pairs of hands are going to be necessary, although I have many memories of shaking like a weightlifter trying to get a large wall upright on my own. Once the wall is in position, fix the wall to the floor using large 100mm x 8mm screws. Remember at this point, and throughout the build for that matter, to check the levels. You should fit temporary wooden stays to hold the wall perfectly plumb. As the wall is free-standing the temporary stays are best left in place until the adjacent walls are ready to be fitted.

Ideally, the next wall to be built will be the opposite wall and this is usually easier to build in situ. This structure will be built in the same fashion as the first wall, that is to say, the framework will be 4in x 2in, braced with 11mm OSB, covered in breathable membrane and battened out ready for cladding. However, it is best practice to now build all walls to a finished framework only.

For this particular example, I will assume the front wall will have doorway access and windows, although they could just as easily be on the side walls. Adjustments will be required in the framework for all openings and, depending on the span of these openings, they may require lintels above the door or window frames to help support the roof weight. This is especially important for large spans, such as you get with bi-folding doors, or if the roof is to carry substantial weight, such as a green roof – if you have any doubts then it would be wise to consult a structural engineer. Once again, use a temporary brace to ensure the wall stays vertical until the side walls are in place.

The remaining two side walls can now be built, again following the same instructions as the previous walls. The temporary stays should be carefully removed ensuring the existing walls remain plumb and the side walls can be fixed in place and securely fastened to the existing walls using appropriate screws.

CASE STUDY

The Little House Shed
Approximate size: 11.25m²

The Brief

This little shed was designed and built for my parents. The concept was to create a multifunctional shed that was in keeping with a 1920s house and garden. The shed needed to make use of a dark, unused and overgrown corner of the garden. The shed was also going to act as a little outside version of the house and had to be adaptable for different uses by all the family.

The Design

Externally, the main focus of the design was to make it fit with the period style of the house and garden, but within quite a tight budget. We wanted it to reference the history of the house without copying it. My mum explains:

'Originally, when these houses were built in the 1920s most of them had a summer house, they were small octagon-shaped structures, but of course after all those years most of them had rotted away. The idea was to replace this original shed.'

We decided quite early on that a little house or cottage would suit its location more than a contemporary design and we felt that a pitched roof with tiles would be the best way to achieve this look. The Little House Shed was to be in a corner and we were aware that once the roof went on, it might be a bit dark inside, so we decided to have two long, thin strips of glass right through the roof.

I tried to mix styles to give the shed personality and also make the build efficient. For example, I used leftover fencing for the side wood cladding, next to a rendered front wall to give it the 'little house' look. The curved front corners referenced art deco buildings, anchoring the shed to the 1920s or '30s, rather than a generic square cottage style.

The dimensions of the shed were defined by an old pear tree and a laurel tree on either side of the footprint. To save money and to some degree to save the trees, we decided not to rip them out, but build between them. The width

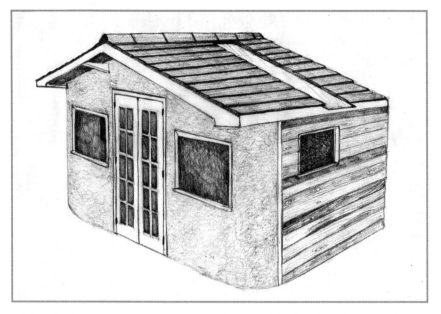

of the shed was just enough to get a full-sized bed in length ways, should anyone want to sleep out there. The height was always going to be tricky because it can be difficult to get it under the UK permitted development height of 2.5m with a pitched roof, but it is possible. It usually means having quite low side walls and a shallow pitch on the roof.

The Build

We decided to put a concrete slab in, partly because it was a damp corner and partly because my uncle does this for a living so he came to help. We hired a mini digger to make the foundations, which my uncle taught me how to use, and I had a lot of fun sitting there one evening moving dirt around until the controls made sense. The build was quite straightforward, with most thought being given to the curved wall corners and the roof structure. For the curved wall corners, I basically drew a circle at the base and followed this line with the framework, I then used a thin ply to create the curve.

Originally, we were going to use slates for the roof, but the concrete tiles were quite a bit cheaper. I was concerned about the amount of weight in the concrete tiles for such a shallow pitched roof, so we decided to use a purling support across the joists. Although this went through the line of the roof windows, the structural integrity outweighed any aesthetic compromises, as it always should. We decided to use ceramic floor tiles inside so it could be easily mopped out because it was always intended to be used in an outdoor environment.

The Finished Build

I can remember the corner of the garden before the shed was used and the building of the shed has made the garden bigger because the previously unused space is now accessible. Internally, the space immediately developed a familiar homely feel, in part due to the family furniture. My nan died around the same time as the shed was finished, so there was furniture in her house that was getting cleared out and, as is often the case, the family didn't have the room for it all. It is nice to keep the furniture going and give it a home, as my mum explains:

'We didn't buy anything for the inside of the shed, most of it came from my mum's house. Some of the reason for building the little house in the first place was to house the things we had. There's a little black, homemade stool in there, my mum bought this from a second-hand shop up the road so it must be about a hundred years old. When we were children we would use it as a little table or sit on it by the fire, it doesn't seem right to just get rid of these things.'

The shed has given the family a fearless outlook towards the garden space, by this I mean they will be out there for all occasions knowing that if the weather turns they can simply move into the little house for shelter and carry on. It especially works well for my parents who were immediately at ease with the shed. Although the shed is in a dark corner, the light it does

receive is at crucial parts of the day when the shed gets used most often. My mum also tries to connect the shed with the garden space by changing it throughout the year:

'I would also say it gives me a chance to have a creative outlet. We change the "little house" with the seasons in the same way the garden changes. Things like changing the colours from light, fresh spring tones to russets and oranges for autumn or using fairy lights and a Christmas tree to make it cosy for Christmas or taking the curtains down to let light in for the summer months. It's especially peaceful out here in the summer. I will often sit out here with a cup of tea and watch the birds on the feeders as the sun goes down.'

It is clear that my parents have affection for these types of small outdoor builds because of the places they grew up in. It is not always memories of gardens or countryside retreats that conjure up the childhood experience; we can have just as much nostalgia for small urban spaces. My mum remembers her own childhood shed:

'The house we grew up in had a brick air-raid shelter in the backyard and my uncles built a wooden shed between it and the house. The other yards in the street didn't have a shed, so we would put concerts on and the other children would walk up the alley and come and sit on the back wall to watch the

show. We had an old wind-up gramophone with a 78 record of 'She Wears Red Feathers and a Hula-Hula skirt'. We were only about six or seven, we would use the air-raid shelter as our dressing room and make our entrance through the shed door dressed as hula girls and dance.'

For my dad growing up, having any kind of a shed was just not possible because they didn't have a yard space, so having a shed was something you aspired to (it's starting to sound like a Monty Python sketch). He does however have memories of the urban chicken sheds that had continued after the war and the pigeon sheds in the local area:

'We always wanted a shed but we lived upstairs in what was called a scotch house which was basically a living room, a bedroom and a kitchen; there were six of us living there. Our yard was a 6in x 3in floating walkway which was just a path to the outside toilet. When we were growing up, people who had sheds usually had them for pigeons, you could always tell because the pigeons would sit on the top of their roofs. If they were racing pigeons, they lived in better conditions than the people. I used to work with a fella who would win pigeon races. He would carefully polish all the corn piece by piece so they had the best food and he always said he had the same shed roof for years because the pigeons used to recognise it and when he moved house he took the roof of his shed with him.'

Conclusion

As I look at the shed now from the dining room of the house, it nestles neatly into the corner of the garden and the style of the 'little house' fits with its surroundings. Because the build was for my parents I have a good understanding of how the shed has changed their lives and what has worked well and what they would change with hindsight. The changes they would have made are, on the whole, small things. My mum would've had the windows a little lower, so she could see out of them when sitting on the sofa and she would've had bigger windowsills to put plants and candles on them. My dad would've made the shed a little bigger by possibly ripping out one of the trees and hitting the 15m² building control limit. He would have also made the overhang a little bigger so it could be sat under in the rain.

From my perspective, although I understand these changes, they all would have had an impact on how the shed looks. It still feels a good size to be in and I'm not sure if it would have been worth it. However, I do agree that it is worth getting the right size windowsills. Overall, the shed has reconnected the family with a part of the garden that was seldom used, it has given them the confidence to engage in more outdoor social events and it has provided every family member with the means to have some occasional quiet time.

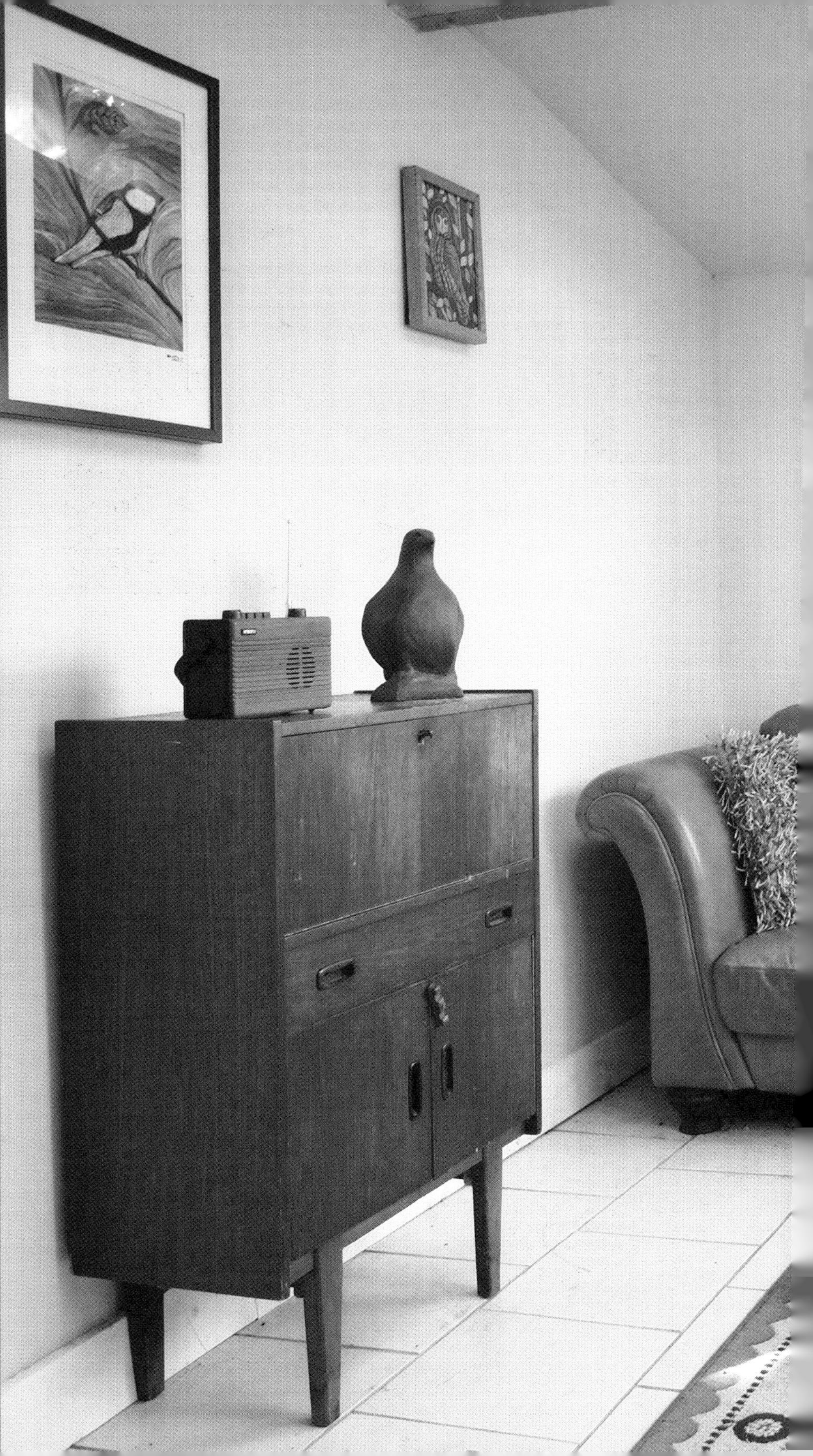

ROOF STRUCTURE

I often say in essence there are only two things you need to be sure of when making a building and they are: a stable structure and keeping water out. The roof affects both of these aspects and therefore is an especially important day's work. Although the rules of building are often simple, there are obviously an infinite number of manifestations and variables based on these basic principles. It is never wise to be complacent when building, but mistakes made when constructing the roof can be especially costly. The roof needs to be right as it is protecting the whole of the build from weather. It is also important to remember that there is often a lot of weight in a roof and the forces upon it will be acting perpendicular to the direction the wood has grown, for this reason you need to take some time to understand weight and span ratios.

Without going into elaborate roof designs there are two basic structures: either a flat roof or a pitched roof. Each has its own merits and, to a lesser degree, its own disadvantages. There are also many choices of finish. The decisions you make about your roof are determined by aesthetics, structural integrity, location, climate and costs.

The Flat Roof

For efficiency reasons, the first and most usual choice at present is a flat roof. This is probably the easiest in terms of construction, the least expensive and fits with many modern designs. The flat roof is also often the most practical when shed building because it maximises the volume of the space while following the rules of the permitted development height restriction.

The choices of watertight finishes have moved on since the days of difficult torch-on asphalt sheeting. If a torch-on felt roof is a requirement, these days it will probably be because of price, nevertheless, it should always be installed using an approved fitter.

Although termed 'flat roof', a flat roof does in fact run or slant in one direction. The run will often be from front to back to maximise the front height and allow more room for a door and also because the sometimes unsightly guttering can be hidden at the back of the build. The most common reasons for the roof gradient to slant towards the front are because there is a problem installing guttering at the back or because a green roof is being installed and you want to see the plants.

The fall on a flat roof should be sufficient enough to drain rainwater away quickly so as not to allow pooling or build-up of silt, but at the same time not too quick so as to leave behind dust and leaves. To a point, this will be decided by the choice of roof finish so it is always worth familiarising yourself with the manufacturer's instructions before finalising the structure. The usual fall required is between 1:40 and 1:80, but this does differ depending on the choice of the finished material. For example, if a green roof is the required finish then this should be pitched at a fall of no less than 1:60, whereas some metal roof manufacturers will insist on 1:80.

There are two methods of achieving this roof fall. The first is to have firrings cut at the required incline using wood that is the same width as the roof joists, then fitting the firrings directly on top of the joists before fixing the wooden panels. The advantage of this method is that it leaves a flat ceiling on the inside of the building. However, it does add extra costs by having the firrings made and fitting them. The other option is to build one wall higher in the first place and sit the joists directly on the wall plates. This will achieve the correct fall without

the use of firrings, but will also give an interior ceiling with the same pitch. This is my preferred method because again it will maximise the headroom.

The roof joists used will sit directly onto the wall structure and the size of these joists will be determined by the overall span. As a guide, grade C16 6in x 2in is sufficient up to a 3m span set at 400mm centres (see tables at the back of book). This method is suitable for all flat roof systems. However, if a green roof is intended then it is always recommended to check specific manufacturer's specifications as there are many lightweight green roof systems available that will help you keep your roof joist size to a minimum, but you will pay more for these lightweight systems.

When the roof framework is securely fixed to the walls, noggins made from the joist off-cuts should be fitted between each joist to correspond with the roof board edges. These noggins not only add lateral strength, they also add strength to the roof board edges. The best choice of roof boards is 18mm external ply. In most cases, the roof boards should be firmly screwed down to the joists using countersunk screws and any indents filled with wood filler. If, for any reason, the finished build at this point is to be left overnight, then the roof should be temporarily covered with a waterproof sheet.

My choice of roofing system is usually an EPDM rubber roof because of its versatility and ease of fitting. More often than not, the roof will not be visible so how the rubber looks next to the wooden cladding is not usually a problem. The rubber roof is an extremely watertight solution, it can be ordered to fit the roof in one piece and it usually comes with a minimum 20-year guarantee. It is also possible to purchase a thicker rubber for use underneath a green roof system. A rubber roof can be self-fitted with minimal skills and there should be a selection of additional extras, such as edges and flashing systems from your supplier.

There are, of course, many other choices of finished solutions for a flat roof, including metal sheets of varying styles and colours, fibreglass/plastic kits, and self-adhesive shingles to name but a few. If the choice is a sheet metal or plastic cladding system, then it is also worth considering a pre-insulated solution. Again, these pre-insulated systems come in a variety of styles and colours and although they are relatively expensive, they have the advantage of eliminating the plywood roofing sheets. They also come with a finished interior surface (white), removing the need for an interior ceiling.

The Pitched Roof

When considering a pitched roof, an important factor in your decision should be its finished overall height, especially if the construction is to be built within the rules of permitted development. This height restriction will have repercussions on the design. For example, the rules of permitted development in the UK often restrict overall height to just 2.5m and at this height the subsequent side walls would be too low for a door.

However, pitched roofs do offer many other advantages. These include ensuring that there is less perpendicular load on the roof which means a smaller timber size, better flow of water, and, if done properly, probably less need for maintenance. It is also often easier to fit a roof window, such as a Velux, in a pitched roof. The usual requirements for such windows are a minimum angle of 30 degrees. You should also consider the cost – a pitched roof will almost always be more expensive because of the extra labour framing out the structure and laying the roof tiles. In my experience, the most common reason for making the decision is an aesthetic one (for sheds); if you want that cottage look then a flat roof will just not do the job.

If the final decision is to go with a pitch, then there are basically two methods of construction: rafters or trusses. Trusses are a pre-built triangular frame that has the advantage of being built at ground level then lifted into position to be fitted at roof height.

Often 4in x 2in timber will be used for the construction of trusses, but this is dependent on the span of the roof and the weight of the tiles. It is sensible to make the first truss and check it in position, assuming it fits then you can use it as a stencil to make all subsequent trusses. Detailed truss plans can be easily found online.

If the choice is to use rafters, again you are constructing a triangular shape but the separate rafters are fixed straight onto the roof between the wall plate and a ridge beam. You will need to make an accurate plumb cut at the ridge and a bird mouth cut to sit on the wall plate. Start with the two sets of rafters at the far ends of the roof and once the ridge is fitted, the remaining rafters can be added. The thickness of wood used is again based on the span and the weight of the roof, but 4in x 2in is commonplace. Throughout the construction, ensure the ridge remains perfectly central and level. If a canopy or front overhang is required, then the easiest method is to extend the top wall plate to the size of the required canopy and use this as the starting point.

If you are in doubt about the structural strength of the roof due to a large span or heavy tiles, then it may well be worth considering fitting a purlin. A purlin or purlin plate is a wooden beam that runs horizontal at right angles to the rafters and is usually supported by end posts or directly on the gable structure. Remember the purlin may be visible from the inside which in turn may affect the interior design, but I personally like to see some wooden structure in a build, it gives it a certain integrity.

With the roof structure now in place, the next stage is to cover it with a thick breathable membrane. Again, stretch the membrane from side to side starting at the bottom and work up to the ridge with the recommended 150mm overlaps. When the whole roof is covered, roof batten are fitted horizontally to the rafters. The distance between these batten is determined by the tiles to be used. These batten are not just for the fixing of tiles, they also secure lateral movement of the rafters and help ventilate the roof structure. At this point, the structure is temporarily watertight but you should aim to get the roof completely finished sooner rather than later.

Decisions on the finished look of a pitched roof will probably be dependent on surrounding buildings and the need to blend in. However, there are a lot of choices when it comes to style and budget, ranging from slates to clay tiles to corrugated metal sheets, all of which when fitted properly do the job equally well.

CASE STUDY

The Square Window Shed
Approximate size: 15m²

The Brief

The concept was to create a relaxing space that would increase the square footage of a one bedroom London flat and re-engage the clients, Mark and Laura, with a tired and seldom-used garden space. The build needed to have sleeping facilities and they were keen that it should be in some way personal to them; they also wanted to use some recycled materials to give the shed character.

The Design

Mark and Laura live in a good-looking 1930s house in London, but like so many in the city, it has been split into an upstairs and a downstairs flat. The high house prices in their area has made recreational space a luxury. They like the area in which they live but in order to stay they needed more space and not just more, but better space. Laura explains:

'We wanted an extra lounge that felt like our own, to do what we want in and we needed a place for friends and relatives to sleep, so they would feel private and free to do what they want. We also wanted somewhere to just sit and relax and be in the garden, because we like our little flat and we really didn't want to move.'

It was important to use the full width of the garden to maximise the build because a lot was being asked of the shed space, but at the same time we didn't want to encroach on their relatively small garden. The idea was to create a courtyard between the house and the shed. The size and shape of the build was also determined by the length of wood I could physically fit through the house.

They had been given a lovely door for free and to move away from that bi-fold doors look, we decided to use irregular-shaped smaller windows to give it a more unconventional, personal character. Concerns about the amount of light that would come into the space were addressed with one

large window that mirrored the door. Mark and Laura were keen to finish the shed to quite a high standard but they had set a budget. My advice was to go for a few well-thought-out design aspects and ideas, such as the feature windows, a bed storage solution and beautiful reclaimed materials.

The Build

This shed turned out to be a very efficient build, sometimes it's not always obvious why, although the build was all the more interesting since there were considerable obstacles along the way. I remember there was a right angle just as you walked in through the front door followed by another turn into the kitchen. Since there was no access around the back, I had to carefully measure what lengths of timber would fit through the house. A 3.6m length of 4in x 2in fitted to the millimetre but only by twisting it back and forth at various points without damaging their plaster work. It was a bit like some gigantic buzz wire game. The first week of the build was also filled with biblical thunderstorms and I have a clear memory of desperately sweeping away water from the build as the heavens opened. Still, once the structure started to take shape, things changed and everything went perfectly.

Part of this I attribute to the communicative working relationship we had, which generated quick and good decisions; it also helped that although they changed their minds on occasion, they always had their choice of materials on site and ready to go on schedule so it didn't hold me up. Laura remembers her first visit to the reclamation yard:

'We changed some things and made things up as we went along. Originally we wanted blackened larch or pine, but we decided it was too close to the house, and might look too austere. Then I saw the reclaimed cedar and the reclaimed gym floor. My friend had put gym flooring right through the downstairs of their house. I've always loved it and I thought, I might not be able to have it through my house, but I'm going to have it in my shed, and why wouldn't you have a maple floor? It's beautiful.'

When the reclaimed 90-year-old cedar arrived on site, one side had been planed to a finish that had come up really well, but I actually preferred the rough side with dents and colour changes – I thought it told the story of the wood. I ran it by Laura who eventually agreed. It is not always easy to make a decision like displaying an unfinished surface, but this confident step moved the shed away from the ubiquitous look they were so keen to avoid.

The insulation is worthy of a short mention. We used a denser Rockwool in the wall cavities and then a 25mm layer of insulating board over the whole of the walls and ceiling before the plasterboard. It's an easy way to get a really good result.

The Finished Shed

I revisit this shed on a chilly autumn morning. As I stand inside the first thing I notice is how warm it is, it is so luxurious and cosy. The shed feels separate enough but at the same time there is a dialogue with the house via the courtyard area between them. The level of finish the shed has fits the

house and this is something Mark and Laura were conscious of as Mark recalls:

'We never did it to make money, but we knew we weren't going to lose out, so we were happy to put money into it. We saved up to do it properly, so we wanted to spoil ourselves. The space was special so we bought things that we really wanted and we thought needed to be in here like the iMac and the mid-century chairs. The place was so beautifully crafted, we wanted to do it justice.'

Conclusion

From my perspective, the three main elements we chose to put time into have worked really well. The bed storage is basically a mattress-sized box that reaches the ceiling. The flooring continues up the wall of this box and is an interesting change from the usual plasterboard finish. The bed is not used often, so the use of a foldout bed would have been an unnecessary expense and would have been less flexible – it's a simple solution to the problem and there's nothing wrong with that. I also think the windows work well; they feel quite playful especially the little window down the bottom for the cat to peer through, and with the addition of little cacti and ceramics, they also feel quite personal and bespoke. I actually used the same proportions as the little panes of glass in the door to help give the eye a subconscious sense of overall structure. Although the shed feels high quality, for Laura it has that elusive feeling of character that only the smell and bashed-up surfaces of reclaimed wood can achieve:

'Wooden buildings smell really nice, they have that warm smell. My great aunty Marge had this gorgeous summer house. I used to love playing there, it had a veranda on the front and a place you could go and sleep above. Sitting here talking to you now, I can still smell what it was like. I used to love it, it gave you this nice feeling because it was outside. This place stayed with me and I think I always wanted something like this.'

I can see that they both love the space and they are using it in the way they intended. They have both put their own stamp on the build, with Laura's grassy planting and bits between the windows and Mark's home-made little sleeping den for the cats. A build like this has the ability to transform a small property and subsequently transform the way they feel about the place they live. Mark sums it up nicely:

'The shed makes me smile. Peace and tranquillity are things you crave being a Londoner; if you have something nice to look at and be in, it makes a real difference. I actually get excited about coming home now, it makes me feel relaxed in my own house, finally! When you come in here, you're in your own little world, like a little cocoon, it feels good for you. There's another dimension to it. Instead of being in two minds whether were going to move, I now feel more settled.'

CLADDING

Cladding has the greatest impact on the look and feel of your shed because, more often than not, it is the prominent visible material. It also has the dual purpose of protecting the shed from the weather and creating finished edges for elements such as windows, door frames and fascias. The type of cladding, its colour and its texture will all have a bearing on the personality of your shed, for this reason you should carefully consider your options. The cladding you choose will also have an impact on how long it will take to fit. Generally speaking, cladding days feel like a second-fix job as more accuracy and patience is needed in order to achieve a suitable quality of finish.

When cladding a shed, the decision will usually be made on aesthetic preference according to design and cost because most modern methods of cladding should be sufficiently watertight. There are many different materials and fitting techniques, but for the purposes of the shed it is still various types of wood that are understandably the most popular choice. Apart from being watertight, the cladding should be aesthetically suitable

– it should be influenced by the surrounding architecture and environment by either reflecting a similar style or offering a well-thought-out contrast to it. Think also about whether the cladding on the walls will be different to that on the roof or fascia and whether it will match the chosen doors and windows.

The choices in the types of wood used for cladding are plentiful and the price variation between these different woods is considerable. The available budget will of course have a major impact on your decision, but my advice is to try and squeeze together the budget for your preferred choice of cladding because it has such a substantial influence on how the shed looks. Sometimes it is possible to use a cheaper cladding for the back

and side walls, especially if these walls are not to be seen, either way, my opinion is that wood from a sustainable source should always take priority.

In my experience, the most popular choices for cladding are pine, cedar and larch, although this is dependent on the location of the build and the subsequent availability of the various wood types. Some woods are more suitable for cladding than others largely because of the climate the species of tree has evolved in and the resultant difference this causes.

Types of Wood Cladding

Scots Pine *Pinus sylvestris (Pinaceae)*

The genus *Pinus* is made up of evergreen trees that are found in temperate regions in the northern hemisphere. It is the most economically important genus of conifers in the construction trade, predominantly because they are fast growing softwoods that can develop in relatively close stands. There are somewhere in the region of 126 species of pine, a good representative species would be Scots Pine of which a large volume of lumber is produced in Scandinavia. Typically, the heartwood is pale reddish-brown and clearly distinct from the paler, creamy-white to yellow sapwood. The wood is resinous and knotty, and its texture may be fine or course, depending on its origin. All pines have a lot of resin canals. The word 'Pine' is in fact derived from Latin *Pinus*, which can be traced to the Indo-European base pit 'resin' (source of English pituitary). The wood is soft, medium in weight and density, with good strength properties. Pine is not a durable wood, and is vulnerable to the weather and to insect attack, for this reason, it must always be treated in some way if used for cladding.

Western Red Cedar *Thuja plicata (Cupressaceau)*

Cedar is a very popular choice for cladding, in recent times it has been perceived to be compatible with contemporary design. There are many different types of cedar. It is generally considered that Western Red Cedar, grown in Canada, is the superior wood for cladding and is therefore often more expensive. In fact, Western Red Cedar is not a true cedar at all. It is classified as being 'softwood', yet offers most of the advantages of much heavier hardwoods. It is often clean and knot-free and enjoys a natural resistance to moisture absorption and decay, meaning it can usually be installed without further treatment. Cedar is among the most stable of softwoods, giving the advantage of very little post-fitting movement. When newly cut, the heartwood can vary from salmon-pink to dark chocolate-brown. It ages to a reddish-brown colour and, if left untreated, will weather to a silver-grey. Because it is relatively low in resin content, it is an ideal choice for staining or painting.

European Larch *Larix deciduas (Pinaceae)*

Another popular choice is Larch of which there are many species including European, Western, Japanese and Siberian. Larch is, in fact, a deciduous tree which is unusual for a conifer. It tends to vary in grade because it can be prone to knots. The higher the grade the less knots and the easier to work, although the knots tend to be tight and small, but this varies between the different species. Larch ranges from reddish-browns to golden-browns and changes to a muted grey tone over time. Siberian Larch is popular with architects because of its increased heartwood, which comes from its slow growth in a cold climate and which gives it a superior quality. Larch is generally considered hard-wearing but also flexible in thin strips; it is more durable than most conifers. Its high density means it is more difficult for decaying organisms to penetrate the wood and this resistance to rot makes it good for posts or fencing as well as cladding.

I personally find it fascinating to read about the specific properties of different tree species. It is absolutely worth considering any wood that happens to become available and with a little research you can easily find out if it will be suitable. For example, if budget is less of a concern, then consider the temperate hardwoods – Oak and Sweet Chestnut being especially hardy. Green Oak will naturally weather as it ages to

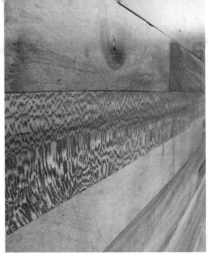

a lovely silver grey and blend in to most environments. It also has the advantage of requiring no further maintenance for anything up to 100 years, which makes it ideal for hard-to-access areas. Sometimes a wood can be difficult to identify, especially if it has been sourced from a reclamation yard, I have used many exotic and tropical woods that have been ripped out of old buildings, but I strongly advise if you are buying these hardwoods from new that you avoid the support of illegal deforestation and buy them from sustainably managed forests.

If you can source a tree locally then this is an ideal scenario in terms of the environment. Recently, I clad a shed in London Plane, which was sourced and prepared from a tree that had been felled for safety reasons within a mile of the shed. I found it a beautiful wood to work with and because it was quarter-sawn stock, the many and very clear rays it has give it a distinctive and attractive fleck figuring known as lacewood. This wood is sometimes treated chemically to form harewood, which leaves the flecks in their original colour but turns the background grey.

It is also worth considering thermally modified timber. These emerging processes mean less durable inexpensive softwoods such as pine can be successfully used, with the advantage of sustainability. Think of the process as a sort of extreme heat without catching fire. The high heat modifies the cell structure of the wood and makes it highly resistant to rot while greatly reducing expansion and contraction. First, sugars and resins are cooked out of the wood, leaving nothing for the fungus and bacteria to feed on. Second the components in wood that hold on to water are converted into those that do so less. Since thermally modified wood does not absorb or hold moisture as it would prior to treatment, species that typically do not perform well in outdoor or wet environments can now be used as cladding. As well as enhanced physical properties, the treatment also results in a consistent deep brown tone.

There are different profiles and finishes of cladding, which are particularly affected by how the cladding will join together. The main choices are: feather edge, shiplap, tongue and groove, and square edge, all of which can be fitted horizontally or vertically. In any event, do not buy wood that is too thin as it can prove to be an uneconomic choice in the long run.

Feather edge boards are tapered across the width usually from about 12mm to 18mm and are mostly fitted horizontally for maximum weather protection. You should fix the cladding to the batten from the bottom and work up overlapping the thin edge with the thick edge by at least 25mm. This choice of cladding produces an appealing rustic style ideal for a traditional or barn look. Feather edge boards can also be purchased with a wavy edge finish to give your build a cabin style.

Shiplap is again usually fitted horizontally because it will have a greater protection against weather. The front face is shaped so that the top of each board fits neatly behind the bottom edge of the adjacent board resulting in a very tidy finish. Because the wood is prepared the finish is less rustic. This clean finish is often copied with plastic claddings. Tongue and groove produces a very uniform, contemporary look. It can be laid equally well horizontally and vertically. It relies not on overlapping planks but the tight fit of a tongue inside of a groove for its weather protection. It is quite common to purchase cedar or larch tongue-and-groove cladding for a sleek, vertically clad build with clean lines.

Square edge also finishes with a neat, uniform style and contemporary look in either direction. Usually boards vary in width between 125mm and 225mm with a thickness anywhere between 12mm and 22mm. As there is no overlap or tongue-and-groove finish then any uneven or damaged edges will expose the joints to weather conditions in relation to the other boards. For this reason, it is often a good idea to have a gap behind the cladding in order for any trapped water to escape. Another good way around this is to double lay, that is to fix a first layer of boards vertically with a gap of about 40mm less than the overall board width, then overlay these gaps with the same width boards by 20mm, this gives a substantial-looking, alternative finish, while increasing the overall weather protection. Whatever method of timber cladding is selected, always make sure enough fasteners are used and pay careful attention to seals around windows and doors.

While timber is the more traditional choice, there are many alternatives now readily available, not least metal or fibre cement products, which can produce a modern look for the design conscious. Metal cladding is usually powder-coated or enamelled steel, zinc or aluminium. All of these come in many designs and colours, they are relatively easy to self-fix and offer excellent weather protection, while more elaborate designs encourage air flow and ventilation. They can be quite costly but they require very little maintenance. Most systems offer interlocking versions that can be fixed horizontally or vertically with the same advantages but they do alter the finished appearance.

Fibre cement cladding is a good cost-effective alternative to both wood and metal. It comes in many finishes and colours, which can be useful when attempting to blend a shed into its architectural surroundings. Fibre cement is a composite material that mimics other natural products in appearance like timber, brick or stone render. It is very durable, hardwearing and lightweight, while being non-combustible. It is easy to cut and self-fix in the same manner as timber on batten or it can be bought as a click-fit system. However, if the build has lots of irregular design, windows and doorways, the cost of specific trim and seals can soon mount up.

I think it is also worth mentioning that basically anything can be used for cladding, granted with lesser or greater degrees of success. I have seen a shed that was clad in tiny mosaic tiles, cut-up yogurt cartons or a mix of old and new recycled materials. Like all building processes, try to keep in mind the principal rules and adapt your material to become compatible. Think of the cladding as the skin of your shed. To keep the skin healthy the water should not collect, it should flow off it (this is further enhanced with airflow which is created by an air gap) and this skin should stay in place with suitable fixings. After this you can let your imagination go to achieve the result you want.

DOORS AND WINDOWS

On the face of it, doors and windows are a means to provide access and light. Their functional essence will always be the primary reason for their existence, but this practical value is not enough to explain their purpose. Doors and windows have the power to change the whole feel of your shed by making it bright and airy or intimate and cosy. They can create a style, perhaps a rustic cabin with a wooden barn door and small cottage windows or perhaps a slick modern design with bi-folds and large mirrored glass. They can bring an aesthetic structure by giving your shed a solid symmetrical order or balance an unusual asymmetrical shape.

Windows

UPVC

Let me rather reluctantly start with UPVC plastic windows. If your shed is being built on a budget and its look is towards the contemporary end of the spectrum, then it may well be that UPVC is the best choice given its ability to meet all modern requirements while not breaking the bank. UPVC comes in many colours, including realistic wood designs, although a standard white finish will invariably be the most economic. They have good, secure locking mechanisms offering overall security and they can be bought ventilated, unventilated, double- or triple-glazed, gas-filled for advanced thermal qualities and so on. It is worth adding that I have on occasion obtained white UPVC windows basically for free because of their propensity to be ordered at the wrong size and thrown away, I have then sprayed them black, making them look similar to a more expensive sprayed aluminium frame.

Aluminium
Aluminium windows offer all the same qualities as UPVC but to my eyes they look better. Although this may be rather subjective, I think most people would consider them to look more expensive. Decisions on whether to purchase aluminium frames usually focus on the balance between aesthetics and cost. Again, it is worth trying to purchase them second hand because people will often replace them.

Wood
A well-made bespoke hardwood window is the ideal and often best-looking choice for any opening window, but you will pay for this luxury. Because of

this cost any second-hand purchase is all the more valuable, but it is worth considering that UPVC and aluminium frames will be virtually maintenance-free whereas wood, especially softwood, will no doubt need more upkeep and may need to be replaced sooner. However, from my perspective, this is often a price worth paying.

Fixed Window.

One often overlooked design choice is the use of 'no dedicated window frames', that is to say, an opening built for glass panels which do not open but are permanently fixed. This method is a cost-effective but highly adaptable form of window making. For example, I have often used this to build a long thin window that sits high above next door's fence, a feature which is especially useful if this is a source of direct sunlight. Glass panels can also be built into walls (and the roof) at generous proportions both vertically and horizontally, giving maximum access to light from all directions. Large

or extreme dimensions such as long, thin glass from floor to ceiling I find sit well in a modern design and contrast against, for example, a rough reclaimed cladding. If you do choose a design such as this, then remember that if the glass is below 800mm from the floor then for safety reasons it must be toughened. Likewise, if glass is fitted as roof panels they also must be toughened. This is a required UK building regulation, but regardless of the glass destination it is a sensible choice. Also, since the windows will not be ventilated, then an allowance may be needed elsewhere for overall room ventilation.

Glass

Glass has made great technological advances in recent years, giving it much improved thermal properties and constructional values. The most obvious choice now is a simple double-glazed solution. However, there are many options here also. If the requirements are for extra energy saving or soundproofing, then you can opt for triple glazing, gas-filled glazing, wider spacing bars and thermal efficient glass.

If you are self-building window frames or fixed openings, then take into consideration that to be efficient double glazing is generally considered to need a spacing bar of 16mm as a minimum, assuming 4mm glass will be used, which leads to an overall glass unit depth of c.24mm. However, if sound prevention is a priority then the bigger the gap, the better the soundproofing will be. You could also consider the use of two different thicknesses of glass as well as an extra-wide space bar. For example, a 6mm and a 4mm glass will produce two different soundwave barriers, resulting in better sound prevention than two sheets of glass of the same thickness. Likewise, if heat loss is the priority then consider triple glazing or gas filling, although the benefits don't always match the expense.

Glass panels in the roof are an excellent idea for extra light, pleasing sky views and just the general feeling of space. The options here are two-fold. You can buy a standard roof window of which Velux is the most common UK option, but others are available. These can be expensive depending on their size but they do comply with safety and building regulations.

The other, more design-friendly, option is to build in your own panels from the outset. This also gives you a much wider choice of glass options, such as self-cleaning whereby a special coating uses rainfall to avoid any build-up of dirt, which is especially useful in areas of limited access. Another advantage is size – potentially the whole length of the roof can be used as a window.

Ventilation

In the past, methods of building, particularly in relation to doors and windows, placed less emphasis on ventilation because it was basically less important as sliding sash windows, wooden doors and framework were usually draughty. However, the recent drive towards energy efficiency, coupled with the technological advances of glazing, has resulted in minimal if any heat loss in new builds. While all this is good for our heating bills and the environment, it can have a negative effect on the internal airflow of our new structures and to some degree our sheds. There are three main choices here. First, since the shed is basically outside, then simply opening doors and windows will immediately bring airflow although it will be uncontrolled and potentially chilly in the winter. Second, you can fit an extractor fan that in turn adds further expense by way of extra electrics and the fan equipment. It will also bring with it a certain amount of noise pollution when running. Third, and perhaps the most practical, is to have trickle vents built in to the chosen window design. Trickle vents are a small open slot cut into the window frame with an open and close cover that allows a permanent measured airflow suitable for the size of the room.

Extra Thermal Qualities

The loss of heat from your shed can be more than 25% through the windows alone and if you add a substantial amount of glass to your roof then this can be considerably more.

With the continuing rise in energy costs and the progress of environmental awareness, it makes sense to give extra attention to energy-efficient glass. Even simple double-glazed units can be as much as 75% more efficient than single-glazed options. There are many products now available which are specifically designed to improve thermal insulation, not least thermal glass types.

The most well-known product in energy-efficient glass in the UK is probably K Glass manufactured by Pilkington. This is most often used as the internal section of a double-glazed unit in conjunction with a specifically designed external glass such as Pilkington Optitherm. Each glass has its own unique qualities which when used together provide an overall excellent thermal unit. The K Glass is used on the inside because its primary function is designed to stop internal heat escaping and return it back to the building, whereas glass like Optiwhite is used as the external sheet because it is extra clear, allowing more light and heat in from the sun. This is just one example of the many choices in thermally beneficial glass, but with a little bit of research you should find a glass that is suitable in your budget range.

You may need to decipher the manufacturer's specifications but, generally speaking, heat loss is measured by the thermal transmittance or 'U value' expressed in W/m^2K, which basically means the lower the U value, the greater the thermal insulation. Also, check out window energy ratings expressed as A+ to G with A+ being the most energy efficient.

Doors

Decisions on your doors, both aesthetically and practically speaking, are subject to much the same reasoning as your choice of windows. Your doors should be chosen to fit with your design and, again, the choices of style and material are many including UPVC, aluminium, wood, composite and glass.

Again, the advantage of UPVC over other modern door systems is usually cost. They are invariably cheaper than aluminium while not losing any security or maintenance benefits. The disadvantage to most people will be appearance. Although all systems have a long, low maintenance lifespan, UPVC has a slight edge in its durability. Aluminium doors are a good-looking alternative, but you will pay extra for these looks especially for modern double-glazed units and they can degenerate over time, but in terms of security they can be almost indestructible. From my perspective,

if cost is not an issue then a good temperate hardwood system is hard to beat. To my eye they are the best looking of the doors and the nicest to handle, and systems with modern treatments can potentially last as long as both UPVC and aluminium, while staying in keeping with countrified or traditional environments. Remember also to take into account the possibility of conservation areas, in which case planning will almost certainly mean at the very least aluminium but more probably timber.

Composite doors are a mixture of UPVC, fibreglass and timber, usually cut from a timber/fibreglass 'slab' and framed in UPVC, which results in a more pleasing wide look than UPVC while retaining the strength and security benefits. Often a good wood-effect composite door is hard to distinguish from wood, yet they are supplied with enhanced multi-point locking systems. They can, however, be quite expensive.

In terms of insulation and soundproofing, it largely depends on the type of design. If you choose doors with a large glass area, the results will be similar; again UPVC wins out in relation to value for money. If sound insulation is of specific importance, my advice is to choose a solid wood door with specialised compressible door seals.

Over the years, the perceived standard contemporary design would often include bi-folding doors that open up the whole front of the shed. These are still probably the best way to connect the interior of your shed to the outdoors, but they are expensive and I will sometimes suggest using large double doors fitted with parliament hinges that allow the doors to open flat against the exterior shed wall.

As always, it is worth considering second-hand doors. Besides the environmental benefits, buying second hand will not just save you the cost of the unit, but if the doors are there before the build starts, then the shed can be framed out to the door size which will be more efficient.

It may well be that a second-hand front door picked up for £20 is the perfect choice for your shed or equally a £3,000 set of bi-folds – what's important is that you take some time to consider all your options carefully. Remember that the doors and windows are probably the parts of your shed that you will use the most often and for this reason you should give them the attention of both your thoughts and your finances. It's always disappointing to see a lovely working shed and a rickety old door that needs to be yanked open every time it is used. Each day that you enter your shed, your doors and windows are the starting point to this most wonderful and personal of places, so make this beginning a happy one.

WATER SYSTEMS AND DRAINAGE

Protection from water is one of the first principles of building and the control of this water will help define whether your build has been a success or not. It is often the case that a great deal of time will be taken in designing a hi-tech multipurpose build, while little or no thought is given to drainage and the immediate surrounding area. It can be irritating and quite depressing to see a beautiful summer house with a waterlogged approach that results in muddy shoes dragging a wet garden into a once beautiful interior.

In principal, drainage begins at the roof. The bigger the roof, the more rainwater will need removing. If the roof is an apex design then the amount of water removal is in effect halved, in that the total square area will be dispersed in two directions equally, whereas a flat roof disposes of all the water in one direction, which in turn may require a bigger drainage allowance.

A flat roof will usually drain towards the back and the chances of the back wall being close to an existing party wall are high. If this is the case, it is important not to allow the rainwater to drain straight off the roof edge, because this will inevitably cause problems of damp to the rear wall or at the very least upset the neighbour. The best solution here, regardless of roof type, is to fit a gutter, usually 100mm half round or square UPVC will be sufficient, especially if it is not visible.

The gutter should be fitted with a stop end and an outlet at the opposite end. Fit the stop end first, as high as possible below the roof edge and allow a minimum fall of approximately 10mm per 5m run. Fix the holding brackets at a maximum distance of 800mm apart. Run the outlet to a suitable downpipe with the use of angle fittings if needed, then fit the downpipe to your preferred method of drainage. If you wish to bring the outlet to the front of the build, then the guttering will just continue around the corner or corners following the same rules of fall.

The ideal solution for drainage, particularly on a small roof, is to use a water butt as this will give a supply of stored water for garden use. Try to buy a decent quality and size with a tap outlet and raise the butt above the ground at least to the height of a bucket or watering can for ease of use.

If a butt is not possible or not preferred, then the rainwater will need to be drained into the ground with the use of a soakaway. First, check the drainage quality of the surrounding ground. If the ground has a high clay content, then the drainage will be more difficult. It is easy to check this by digging a hole about 300mm across by 300mm deep and filling it with water to see how quickly it disappears. The quicker the dispersal, the smaller the soakaway needed. The best method of soakaway is to dig a hole about 300mm away from the building measuring about 500mm across by 500mm deep, line the hole with a one-piece weed control fabric and fill the hole with ¾in clean stone. Run the outlet pipe directly to the soakaway and water will disperse cleanly without mess.

Guttering and downpipes come in many designs, sizes, materials and they play an integral part in the overall shed design. The most common is UPVC, this comes in several colours though black, white and brown are the standard so these should be relatively inexpensive. Plastic guttering also comes with different profiles, half round, square and various Victorian-inspired designs, OGEE with a cast-iron effect being a common and realistic example. If budget is less of a problem, then all the same choices are available in powder-coated aluminium both extruded to fit or supplied in set lengths.

Another solution is to use copper guttering. The most common scenarios in which I will use copper are if the roof is slanting towards the front of the build and the guttering will be on show. Copper guttering is usually connected by drilling small holes and riveting it together. It is better looking than plastic, but do remember when considering the aesthetics of your design that the copper will oxidise and turn green-blue in colour unless specifically treated to stay in its original state.

If you really do not want to use guttering to take the water away from your roof, it is possible to allow the rainwater to fall from your roof into a drainage channel in the floor. The principle is basically the same as roof guttering but it is underground.

POWER SUPPLY

One of the most significant changes in modern shed design is the use of power to make it a more comfortable and usable place. In the past, the shed became more and more redundant as winter approached and any aspirations of working while sitting in an increasingly cold and dark environment with freezing hands would soon fade along with the light.

The vast majority of sheds I build these days have a power supply and the various manifestations of this power will always work more successfully if you plan their uses and locations early.

Present UK building laws insist all electrics must be fitted by a qualified electrician and must be strictly adhered to. However, it does no harm to plan your electrics in advance yourself. I usually advise making a scaled drawing of the internal space so you can understand where the various sockets and lights are going to be most useful. Similar planning will be useful for the broadband connections, integrated speaker systems or projectors.

By doing this, you will be more able to discuss the requirements with your electrician. This should be done before any internal fixtures, walls or the ceiling boards are fitted. You should also discuss whether the power source will be from an original supply, usually the house, or from an independent source such as solar panels or perhaps a mixture of both.

If you are using a mains supply, in most cases the electrician will be looking for the most efficient route from the consumer unit in your house, to a small consumer unit in your shed. A channel will be dug from the house to the shed in which an armoured cable will be placed, the thickness of which is dependent on the distance it is has to travel. Your electric power will now be sourced from the shed consumer unit.

Solar panels are an excellent eco choice, but they may not be suitably efficient in the winter months if you are going to need a lot of power. However, solar panels will continue to develop and they become more efficient every year. Solar energy should not necessarily be dismissed even in a colder climate. It is not too difficult to fit a dual system that switches from the original mains source to the solar panels when either less power is needed or the summer months are sufficient to supply the needs.

Solar lighting will run comfortably on a 12 volt system. If the intention is to use electric sockets from solar panels then the input will need to be increased from 12 volt to the voltage of the equipment (240 volt in the UK). The easiest method here is to use caravan/leisure batteries, which are designed to run flat and continually recharge, but again battery technology has developed dramatically in recent years and it will continue to do so. The batteries can be wired in parallel or series and used with a suitable sized inverter to increase the socket mains to the required voltage.

Whether you are using a mains supply or solar, the most common choices for lighting are a pendant, recessed down-lights, spotlights or up-lighting. A pendant light is often sufficient in terms of brightness to light a shed room, and a chandelier or a retro wire and Edison bulb can make it

suit your chosen decor. If you decide you need more light, spotlights are a simple solution when compared to down-lights, as they have just one feed but multiple lights which can be angled to face the direction you want. Down-lights and spotlights are also going to help avoid the low ceiling light collisions with your head. It is actually not uncommon for my builds to have no wiring for lights in the ceiling, people are much more likely these days to use up-lighting and task lighting that simply plug into designated sockets.

When it comes to sockets, one in each corner of the shed room is a good place to start, but it is important to take some time to plan out the interior of your shed and understand how it will be used. It is never worth being frugal with sockets. However bad you think they look, they will not look as bad as an entanglement of extension leads strewn about the floor. For example, if you have a designated desk area, think about the equipment that you have and that you will potentially have in the future. There are also more types of sockets on the market these days, so as well as colours or brushed chrome finishes, options such as USB outputs are now common.

If you can draw even a simple diagram of your expected lighting, sockets and appliances and set up an early meeting with your electrician to talk through any potential problems, this is going to help the whole build go more smoothly.

INTERIOR FINISH

The interior will be the last and one of the more fulfilling parts of the shed build. The interior walls, the floor and any fitted furniture will be the parts of the shed you are in contact with the most, they are a chance to express yourself and make the shed feel like it is yours.

As always, your choices will be dependent on the shed's purpose, but it should also be in some fashion consistent with the original concept of your design. By now you will have a good idea of how your shed will be used, but it can still be useful to 'test out' the function and flow of the internal space before any finishing takes place. Spend a little time in your shed, have one final check to see if your plans for shelf location and desk height are all still good. Make sure you are happy with all the positioning and the amount of both the lighting and the power points. Only when you are completely satisfied should you embark on the final finishing work.

Insulation

Insulation can totally transform any build, but this is especially true of the shed. A space that can be heated within minutes and retains this heat for hours is perceived in a much more favourable light. Cold temperatures can kill the desire to be in a shed and can render the winter shed unusable. The use of good insulation in your shed should be understood as an investment, since the money you will save in heating your shed and the extra use you will get from it will pay you back in no time.

A good place to start is the ceiling. If the budget allows, use a good quality insulation board as most heat loss will be through a poorly insulated roof. Cut the boards accurately to size and fit them tightly between each rafter leaving no gaps. If the depth of rafter allows, insulation boards of 100mm thickness are going to work well. If the budget will not stretch this far then use a mineral wool or fibreglass material, like Rockwool or similar, which can be bought by the roll. If the latter is chosen, always try to use a minimum of 150mm thickness and compress it into place. This is not the most pleasant of jobs, so always wear protective gloves, glasses and a mask, as these materials are an irritant to eyes and skin, and remember to change your clothes and shower before cuddling the baby.

The walls can be insulated in much the same way. If the budget is tight, then it might be worth considering board insulation in the roof and fibreglass or mineral wool insulation in the walls. Of the other types of insulation available, I find sheep's wool to be really nice to use – it is such a pleasure when compared with other insulation materials because it doesn't itch. I also quite often use reflective foil blanket insulation brands. These are relatively easily fitted by basically wrapping up the interior of your shed and taping the joints with foil tape, but keep in mind it will need an air gap to maximise its insulation efficiency. To achieve this you will need to fix a batten frame in place before your plasterboard or chosen finish.

When the insulation is securely in place, the ceiling can be fitted. The most common choice is plasterboard, but before a final decision is made you should have an idea of what is expected from the finish. If your vision is a reasonably conventional design with neat clean lines and a feel similar to most house rooms then plasterboard is ideal.

Plasterboards are very inexpensive and readily available from all building merchants. They come in two general sizes, these are known as 6in x 3in and 8in x 4in, I say this because the more common size in the UK is 900mm x 1,200mm and 2,400mm x 1,200mm. They also come in different thicknesses, the most common being 9.5mm and 12.5mm; although 9.5mm is thinner it is often more expensive because it is less standard. Apart from basic  gypsum plasterboard, there are specific soundboards and time designated fire resistant boards. The larger size boards are obviously much heavier and I would not recommend laying them alone if you are inexperienced. When fitting the boards, screw them directly to the roof rafters and upright joists using 35mm plasterboard screws leaving no protruding edges and making all joins as neat as possible.

At this point you will probably need a plasterer, as attempting to plaster on your own if you lack experience is going to be difficult – especially the ceiling. If your preference is to completely self-build, then the tapered edge boards may well be worth considering to dry line. Dry lining boards have the last few inches of each long edge tapered, these edges meet each other slightly lower than the overall finished board level. The joints are filled using a joint filler, followed by a light sanding down of the edges. This method is preferable for the beginner and the finish is almost as good with minimal practice. The plasterboard can then be painted to the colour of your choice. If you do choose to have the interior completely plastered, you might want to consider leaving the plaster in its raw state and sealing it, this is one of my favourite finishes, but it is not for everyone.

There are many other choices of internal finish. Probably the next most popular is to choose a nice plywood finish. Plywood is a strong, light and versatile material to use. Its strength comes from gluing thin layers together at usually 90 degrees to each other, although some of the more expensive versions can be glued at 30 degrees. Plywood is available in different types of wood and different grades that range from A to D, with D being the lowest quality. Softwood ply is more often considered structural, while hardwood ply is more of an appearance product. Plywood used for its aesthetic quality is generally graded and priced on the quality and thickness of the face veneer. Almost any type of wood can provide the finished veneer surface with the most popular being birch, maple, oak, ash, beech, walnut, mahogany and teak. I would say the most common choice of finishing ply I have used is a 12mm Baltic Birch ply, which gives a nice smooth, pale veneer and is a good, strong yet light ply.

As well as being easy to fit, ply is a relatively inexpensive way to create modern and warm-looking interior walls. It can also be extended to the ceiling and floors. Floors in ply are less forgiving because the layers that make up the ply are so thin, so it is difficult to re-sand them to bring them back to life. The best advice I can give for your floor is to choose a hardwood veneer and a hardy polyurethane finish to give it the best chance.

Besides the obvious aesthetic quality, a smoother ply is good on walls because you will be brushing up against it. The cost of using a better quality ply is to some degree offset against a cheaper plasterboard interior because there is no sanding or decorating. If you want to seal the ply, be aware that, generally speaking, oil-based treatments may yellow over time compared to water-based ones. Plywood is also a good choice of finish for any curved surfaces.

To fit the plywood is much the same principle as fitting the plasterboard, in that it will need to be cut to the right shape and dimension of the walls and ceiling. It is quite a bit more difficult because you cannot just fill any mistakes with plaster. For this reason, I will often mix the use of plasterboard and a nice plywood. This also breaks up the internal textures and, in my opinion, it gives the shed an extra feeling of luxury and personality. I will choose a favourable consistent shaped wall for the plywood so it is easier to fit. Usually the only cuts I make will be where the plywood joins the corners of the room and the ceiling. To fix the plywood,

glue along the areas that will be fixed to the framework and pin them into place with brads or pins.

Just as with external cladding, but without the added jeopardy of ensuring it is waterproof, basically anything can be used to clad the interior of your shed, so let your imagination go. The use of reclaimed flooring or offcuts of different woods can look great – they will just take a little more time to fit but if you do have the time it will add character to your shed.

Seeing the walls and ceiling in their finished state will have transformed your shed and it will hopefully be beginning to express the design concept you had for your space. However, your floor, in its raw 22mm tongue and groove chipboard state, will probably fall short of your aesthetic vision. I personally don't mind the chipboard finish, as I think it can suit certain builds, especially if it is painted. But if chipboard is not for you, then there are a whole host of specialist floor coverings.

As always, depending on its use, your floor can be brick or tiled, it can be carpeted or, if it is concrete, it can be polished. But by far the most popular floor for the sheds I build is a wooden floor. There are various types of wooden floor and these can generally be categorised as laminate flooring,

engineered flooring and solid wood flooring. I probably lay laminate flooring the most; although it is the cheapest version, it is simple to lay and there are various degrees of quality, with the more expensive floors having a thin layer of wood on the surface. Engineered flooring is the mid-range choice, it usually consists of three or four layers of wood glued at right angles to each other in a tongue-and-groove profile. Although it is slightly more

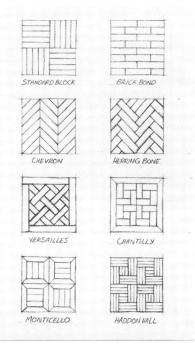

difficult to lay than laminate it is still relatively simple and is less prone to expansion than a solid wood floor.

The solid wood floor is my favourite floor type, but you will usually pay extra because you are basically buying a thicker piece of timber. Solid floors can ultimately be made from any wood type. In hardwoods, oak floors are a traditional standard because they are so hard-wearing and durable. Oak floors also have a pleasing, versatile colour and grain. There are many hardwoods that are in fact much harder than oak, but remember this does not always mean they are more durable. Walnut is a good choice. Although it is softer than oak, it has a dark, rich tone which I think looks luxurious. Other popular hardwood choices are cherry, maple and ash, with bamboo also becoming more common. In softwoods, pine is the standard and for me it works just as well as the hardwoods in a shed, especially if you can pick up an older reclaimed pine floorboard. I happen to like the scuffs and dents of time and, because it is solid wood, if it gets too bad you can bring it back to life by sanding and waxing or varnishing.

To lay a solid wood floor it is important to let it acclimatise to your shed, the longer the better but, generally speaking, a week is sensible. You should buy good strong flooring glue and I also fix it into place with brads or pins.

There are a whole host of patterns to follow when laying your floor. They have intriguing names – Herringbone, Swallowtail, Chevron, Monticello, Versailles or Chantilly parquet, the list goes on. Some traditional styles go back a thousand years, some are relatively new, either way it can have quite a dramatic effect on your interior design. The pattern

will emphasise the craft in your build while at the same time feeling like a modern statement, especially if it is a bold design.

Final trimmings such as skirting boards and architraves come in various sizes, materials and designs including wood, plastic, modern and traditional; again, it really depends on the vision you have for your shed, but I find keeping things simple in a small space works best. If you can make you own skirting from some of the materials you have used, for example, a simple square pine skirt or ripping down your external cedar cladding for window edging, then it will give a familiar consistency to your interior.

With the ceiling, walls and floor now covered, you are within touching distance of your shed becoming a usable space. As part of your overall design there may well be some bespoke elements in the internal structure. The most common bespoke items are shelving and some kind of desk or workbench. To save room in your shed, it can be a good idea to integrate the shelving into

one of the alcoves of the structural framework. If it is an external wall this may compromise the insulation so either try to use an internal wall if possible or you can put a thin layer of foil behind the shelves.

When it comes to a desk or a workbench, you need to weigh up the costs and the time needed to build a bespoke piece versus one bought from a furniture supplier. The obvious advantage is that you can build a desk or bench to perfectly fit a specific place, perhaps the full length of a wall or a unit that turns a corner. There are many different ways to build a bespoke surface. You may want to use the same cladding as the internal or external walls, especially if there are leftovers; likewise you may be able to use some of the better sheets of plywood if any remain. This surface can be supported with wall brackets or you can make or buy legs. A foldout desk is often really useful in a small space. You can create one with hinged supports that fold out underneath the surface or a really simple method is to use chains that are fixed onto the wall above the desk and hold the desk in place.

CASE STUDY

The Walthamstow Cabin
Approximate size: 14m²

The Brief

The brief was to create a shed that would be a place to escape to, echoing mountain cabins or the deckhouse of a boat. The clients, Will and Sarah, wanted the shed for relaxing and socialising in, and as a place to partake in enjoyable work projects. It should have a wood burner, some bespoke crafted elements and recycled or reclaimed materials to give the shed a feeling of authenticity. As Will puts it:

'The concept was to make a hidey hole, a place that is not the house, somewhere we can get away to. We wanted a fantasy place that would give us that feeling you get when you go on an adventure. We wanted it to feel a bit nautical, or rustic, like something you'd find in the mountains of America.'

Sarah had similar inspirations:

'Will's parents had a beach hut in Walton-on-the-Naze near Clacton. When we first got together, we'd stay the night, it had a big tuck shop-style window and a split door. We wanted the shed to remind us of the special moments we had experienced in our favourite places, not reliving them but reminding us of them.'

The Design

I completely get this idea. Bespoke or crafted elements change the way a place is perceived; they can make it seem older or more connected to time. For me, the shed needed to have a high level of attention to detail in order to create that feeling of authenticity and ultimately this meant designing a relatively simple build so we had some budget left to spend on those details. The garden is south facing, so the shed would have plenty of sunlight. We decided early on to have an American-style porch, and the image of enjoying an early evening glass of bourbon while the sun set seemed to cement the idea. The elements we decided to focus extra time or money on were the porch, a wood burner, the use of good quality wood and some kind of bespoke or hand-crafted carpentry, perhaps a nice floor.

The Build

The garden was relatively small, but the area in which the shed was to be built was covered by raised ground and was not being used. I advised them to have this levelled before we started, so the build would go more smoothly and also to give us more head room because we needed to get it under the 2.5m restriction. Once the base was in, there were some concerns from Will and Sarah about the size of the shed and the amount it encroached on the garden. However, I was keen not to make the shed too small because I felt it would compromise their vision for both the shed and the garden and I also thought at this point it probably looked bigger than it would eventually feel because it included the base of the porch. The building process can be quite daunting especially at the beginning when you can't always imagine what will take place.

I had planned the dimensions to be compatible with standard wood sizes, so the frame and shell went up fast, this left more time and budget to work on the bespoke elements. The build remained open to ideas especially regarding the acquisition of the finishing woods and certain second-hand items, and to their credit Will and Sarah worked hard to get the materials and objects they wanted on site at the right times. The materials included a beautiful barn door, an old ship's porthole, oak decking and some lovely locally sourced London Plane cladding.

'We knew we didn't want a shed out of a showroom, we wanted the real deal. That's why we got the London Plane, we got it from a guy from up the road who used wood from trees that had been felled by the council. All of the cladding was from one tree and this nice patina was created by the way he cut it.'

The Finished Shed

For me, this shed has a great deal of personality and it expresses it both outside and in. It is a contemporary cabin but it has touches of the authenticity Will and Sarah were searching for. The shed connects well with the house, the porch creates that feeling of going to their fantasy place and Will and Sarah's early reservations about the size of the build are now a distant memory:

'We were worried about losing our lawn. At first we thought it was huge, but it fits the space perfectly. In reality, we hardly used the garden and certainly not in the winter, we basically only looked at it through the kitchen window. We'd never sat in this corner of the garden, there was a compost bin and an old tree, nothing else was growing here. When you sit here now, it feels the right size, this is the only bit of the garden that gets the sun and it's so nice to actually use it.'

Internally, the shed feels reassuringly cosy. Will's bourbon sits on the shelf next to the sign from his dad's boat Helga and in the corner of the room is one of his father's old oars. Although the shed is new, the various objects in it that link to their past create a sense of time – there is an antler, an old copper barometer and a photograph of a misty morning at the local canal. This feeling of time entering the fabric of the shed is further enhanced by old-fashioned mid-century Bakelite switches and a vintage Edison bulb with twisted wiring bought from a second-hand shop in Margate. We sit in the shed drinking a cup of mint tea that has warmed on the wood burner reminding them of a recent trip to Marrakesh and Will runs a design idea by me for the wall behind the burner:

'I bought a load of discontinued admiralty naval charts and I wanted to do a collage of them. They all have significance to us; they're places we've either lived in or been to. There are notations on some of them where the admiralty worked out that the next edition needs to be different. I like the notes, it shows they are working charts and not just decorative.'

I happen to absolutely love the idea and more than that, I love the excitement and enthusiasm Will shows for it, it is a sign he cares about his shed. Sitting here with the wood burner firing, it definitely captures that fantasy feeling – it's easy to imagine that we have all just returned from collecting some kindling from the dried out lower branches of a mountain pine tree. The shed feels right in their hands and Will confirms to me that we hit the brief:

'I'm really happy that the dream was realised and I've been meaning to treat myself to a posh new bottle to celebrate on the porch – I did see a rare bourbon called Cabin Still. If the first conversation teleported us to here, I would have thought yes – that's exactly what we wanted! I'm looking forward to our parents seeing it. I think my dad will get it. He's always been into boats and things and camping out. He'll understand the fantasy element of it.'

Conclusion

This is a favourite shed of mine. It can be quite a responsibility to decipher the vision of a client and when you do manage to hit a brief there is a real sense of achievement (and relief). I think the shed captures something of Will and Sarah's interesting and open personalities. The choices they made, such as the herringbone floor, the porthole and the wood burner, have enhanced the build and the objects within it help to bring the escapism that Will and Sarah wanted. Not in the sense that they are running away from anything, but in that this place brings them closer to what is important in life. The shed is about enjoying and celebrating the meaningful times of the past and as Sarah puts it, creating memories in the future:

'It must be like how you feel when you have a holiday home, it's that place you go to escape, but we've got that at the end of the garden now. Already I associate it with a feeling of ironically home, of comfort and being cosy and getting away from it all. So far our memories here are of being happy and excited. We will say to each other these days, let's go home and let's go to the shed. Once we're in here it's a struggle to get back to the house.'

PART 5

THE FINISHED SHED

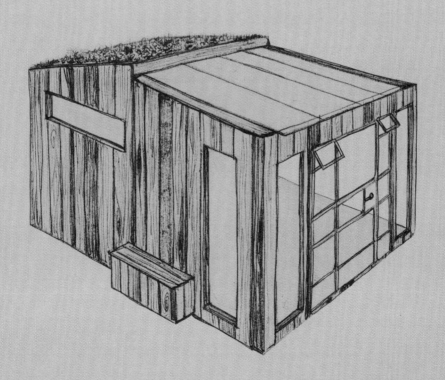

'Real generosity towards the future consists
in giving all to what is present.'

Albert Camus

GETTING TO KNOW YOUR SHED

So, the time has finally arrived when the careful to-scale drawings can be put away along with the tools and your doubts. Your shed is a reality and it starts to gently beckon you from the living-room sofa to the kitchen window to behold it in its magnificence. But at this point your shed is a stranger and the only way to change this is to spend some quality time together.

You should try to get your shed life off to a good start by thanking all the people who have helped bring your shed into existence. Although you have more than likely exchanged money for the labour and expertise that has built your shed, it is never good to see things in life solely from the perspective of monetary value. You should remember it is the hands and muscle of tradespeople that build and it is respectful to appreciate any work done in an autotelic sense, in other words, applaud work for its own sake. This is not only about respect for others, it is about creating the right atmosphere from the very start. If you think well of the people and the relationship that helped build your shed, it will feel a better place to be in. Likewise, if things have gone wrong, let them go, there is no point holding on to any grievances, you don't want any resentment to enter the fabric of your shed's being.

Although your shed can now be considered to be in a finished state, you will originally have had a central concept and it is now time to see that concept right to its end point until your complete vision becomes a reality. This means different things for different sheds.

First, you should respect the new space by buying the things you need to make it function properly. If the shed is an office space, you should buy the computer or install the fast broadband you had promised yourself, if your shed is an art studio you should buy the right easel and the efficient electric wall heater you had researched that will allow you to paint for long periods of time all year round and so on. This is true of aesthetics also. Search carefully for the perfect pair of mid-century modern chairs that will fit your theme; you have after all come this far, don't back out now when you are so close to the end.

Be true to the concept of the shed and remember the purpose for which the shed was designed. All things in life should have a chance to be themselves. I sometimes see a nice old tool in a drawer at a car boot sale, like an animal asleep in the corner of the zoo cage, and I buy the tool just so it can be used even just one last time. If you use the objects that you come into contact with and respect them they will last longer and your life will be all the better for it.

Your shed may look finished and perfect, but you don't want this perfection to move towards a fear of using the shed. Perfection and sheds do not mix well; it is not your house, the purpose of the shed is to give you a sense of freedom. If your shed was designed for planting, now is the time to get the compost out and let it spill through your slatted workbench and miss the bag below and onto your shiny new floor, or if your shed is a writer's den remember creation is king and pin your inspirations into your nice new Birchwood ply.

If the plan for your shed was to use it as a catalyst to change your lifestyle, then now is the time to book in that meeting with your boss. Perhaps your shed was designed to provide you with a means to move to part-time work so you can pursue your dream of writing or painting. Or perhaps once your workshop was finished you intended to make the move to start making bespoke furniture full time, all these things are about seeing that original concept of your shed right through to the finish.

There is also the distinct possibility you will be suffering from a certain amount of building fatigue. There are no rules, you may need to have a break before getting to know each other, but don't leave it too long or it is possible that you will drift apart without ever really understanding what the space could mean to you. Moving into your shed early also lays claim to the space and fends off the greatest threat to all sheds – the storage box.

With even the slightest of lapses in resolve, junk will gravitate towards your shed and once it gets a foothold it will not recover until the biannual tip day comes around. So be strong, remember that in terms of your sense of well-being or your expression of self, your shed may well be of more value to you than your house. If the pressure to use your shed as storage mounts, then maybe it is time to have a clear out or to buy better quality and more versatile equipment to minimise the amount of 'stuff' you have.

One of the best ways to acquaint yourself and others to the joys of shed is to have a shed-warming party. After all, getting to the end of any build deserves a celebration, because all builds involve some kind of sacrifice and need a certain degree of patience and determination. So, whether or not your shed was designed for entertaining, you should absolutely reward yourself with a get-together or a naming ceremony and get involved. My advice is to spend the whole day in there, have some drinks and fall asleep under the workbench – it will do wonders for your shed relationship.

MAINTENANCE

Once your shed is in full flow, you will start to understand how the space works. Perhaps it is everything you imagined it would be and you are using it daily, perhaps you have altered a few things to make it more efficient. Either way, it is important to understand the basic principles of keeping your shed healthy.

The lifespan of your new shed can be dramatically extended with periodic maintenance and repair, with an emphasis on prevention rather than cure. Knowing the expected lifespan of all the products and systems you have used will give you a head start. Ideally, you will have access to the external walls and the guttering but since this is not always the case, you should try to minimise the need for frequent maintenance in the design and build stages.

For the best results, maintenance should be frequent. If you think in terms of keeping your shed comfortable, more a health check rather than curing its illness, it's easier to appreciate the value in confronting problems before they arise. A cold, wet environment along with sudden changes in weather conditions, are the worst enemies of shed health. I sometimes think of buildings in terms of how I would cope with weather, by wearing a good hat, coat and boots.

The Hat

You should keep the roof free from moss, leaves and any unnecessary debris, and check all the various seals for leaks. This not only keeps water from leaking in from above but helps with the efficiency of the roof surface and insulation, especially if the roof incorporates glass panels. Different types of glass will require their own specific forms of attention, even self-cleaning glass needs cleaning, especially in the summer months as the glass technology relies on rainfall to work. A long dry period may result in a build-up of dust and a gentle wash down will keep the glass in tip-top condition. If any panels are of a plastic or polycarbonate type then it is important to not use abrasive products, and follow the manufacturer's instructions.

One of the most commonly neglected maintenance jobs is ensuring gutters are free from leaves and blockages. This is also one of the easiest jobs, as it is a simple matter of getting your hands in and scooping the leaves out. If your gutters block there is the possibility that they will overflow and water could potentially come into contact with your ply roof or even make its way into your build. You will know yourself how your garden acts throughout the year. I usually check my gutters every month just because it is easy since I walk on my roof, but checks are usually going to be most beneficial as autumn creeps in, especially if you are in the vicinity of a large deciduous tree.

When you are doing roof maintenance, always think about safety first. It should be possible to reach most parts of your shed while standing or by climbing onto the roof (I build my shed roofs strong enough to walk on, but you may need to check this). If you are using a ladder, then secure the ladder safely to a good flat surface and secure the top so it cannot move sideways. Don't work above doors and windows unless they are locked, and always remember the three points of contact rule: you should always have two hands and a foot, or two feet and a hand in contact with the ladder. Never work off the top three rungs, which should always be above the point of working.

The Coat

Think of your walls as the coat of the build. You may need to keep the outside walls treated with a good wax or varnish depending on the type of wood cladding you have used. Older oil-based gloss paints tend to be robust but short-lived, constantly needing attention and sealing the surface completely. While this sounds good, it also means any moisture that penetrates the surface remains there, consequently causing much less obvious damage from the inside out. More modern treatments are often water-based, easy to apply and will allow your wood to breathe so any moisture that does penetrate will evaporate in the circulating air. As part of this 'coat' you should check all the windows are closing freely and fitting tight, that your windowsills and seals are clean and working properly, and any air vents are clear.

The Boots

You should check your foundations annually to ensure they are free from any excess ground growth and that any underfloor cross ventilation is still flowing. Ensuring the boots are in good condition will keep the shed on firm ground and will avoid twists or a weakened structure. Try not to stack things against the shed, this will affect everything from ventilation to water tightness and may encourage unwanted growth. Apart from anything else untidiness encourages further untidiness until the shed becomes a dumping ground.

Keeping the surroundings clear by cutting back overhanging trees and tidying grassy entrances will also help. Even the small things will prolong your shed's life, such as oiling and tightening door and window hinges, and wiping away any collected moisture from cold sill surfaces.

While many of these points may seem obvious, they are easily and often overlooked, and problems are not always apparent until it is too late. For example, small roof leaks are often not noticed until damp patches show inside the shed, by which time a minor repair can very quickly become a structural repair. Take care of your shed and have some pride in its appearance and function and your shed will be good to you. By staying ahead of any problems there is no reason why your shed cannot last at least as long as you do.

BEING SHED

It wasn't the easiest of times bringing my shed into existence, a lack of money increased the pressure of the situation. I can recall the early starts, working long physical hours deep into night, but all builds require some kind of struggle. At times, you need a focused determination to push through difficult situations, at others a capacity for thought and patience to solve problems but, like all things in life, it is the struggle that gives you the sense of achievement and makes you care more. As soon as my shed was finished, it was like starting afresh, I had no connection to the hardship. When I think back to the build it is only the sense of purpose that comes to mind, the cold, crisp winter mornings with coffee in hand, a sense that I was working for myself at last. The flaw of a selective memory is one of the great human gifts.

When I began sketching out a rough picture of my plans for an Allotment Roof Shed all those years ago I could never have imagined it would have led to a life that was so involved with these small wooden structures. From winning Shed of the Year to running my own shed-building business to now writing this book, it is absolutely the case that the humble shed has changed my life for the better and it has set my life on a course that is more pleasing and inspiring than it was previously on.

Sometimes it feels as though my shed has been on this journey with me, because it has been such a part of the changes during this time and, like all good sheds, it has adapted to fit my life along the way. I have added many things since it was first built – a wood burner, 12-volt fairy lights, hooks for storage baskets – even for the purpose of writing this book, I chopped down the full-length bench I built for artwork so I could squeeze in a tiny writing desk and shelving for books. Externally the shed is in a constant flux also; each and every year my allotment roof is different depending on what I decide to grow, the sedum guttering, hanging baskets and the blackberries and jasmine that grow up the walls change shape and colour with the seasons. My shed changes with time because it is connected to me and I change with time.

This is true of all sheds and it will be true of yours right from the start. It will quietly creak and relax into position, the floors and pathways will become scuffed and scarred, wood will grey and twist, tiny gaps will

appear into which spiders and other creatures will crawl unbeknown to you. Your shed will gradually become more at ease with itself and you will follow. As you get to know your shed and spend more quality time with it, you will slowly become aware of the little idiosyncrasies that make the shed yours.

In my case, I have affection for these little flaws. I know that I need to leave my wood burner door open because the cowl is too big and on occasion small birds will fly down it. I know in summer that the south-facing succulents will not survive without a little watering, I know when autumn comes I should clean the steps so they don't become slippery and I know that as winter sets in the sun will no longer peek over the neighbours' roof and my solar panel will not be able to sustain my lights. These quirks are the things that make my shed feel like an old friend or family member. The shed is different than the house, it invites introspection – you can confide in a shed because it has a much stronger connection to the real you. When I finally move out of London, it will be my shed which will be hardest to leave behind and I know many others who feel this way too.

This loyalty is born from all the little personal moments spent together. With the physical act of bringing a shed into existence, of changing with it and understanding it over time, and the way we can be ourselves within its walls, we actually develop a relationship with our sheds rather like we do with living things.

Much has changed in my life since that first shed sketch. I have my own family now, I have forged new friendships, I have also lost friends and family. I have noticed over the years that along with its ability to adapt, my shed has provided a constant: it acts as a refuge, it is a place that even seems to have the power to heal. This quality is much more difficult to define, it feels elusive and magical because it is related to our past as much as to the present.

Sometimes I will find myself glancing at the wood cladding on the internal walls of my shed, drifting off to another place. I can see the lines of growth on the wood, the tight grain of successive hard winters; I can see the early exuberant growth when spring appears and then the stronger deep coloured grain of a favourable late summer. I imagine the tree sitting there swaying in a cold Scandinavian wind and my thoughts are no longer so deeply concerned with the solitary world I am in. Wood is unlike other materials and a wooden shed is unlike other buildings because it connects us, we feel a sense of time within it.

The wooden structure has had a special significance throughout our history. It has provided us with shade, shelter and food storage, a place for leisure and for refuge and most importantly it has provided a home and a means to survive. The construction methods and tools when building a wooden structure are largely the same as they always have been and the basic principles of how we understand the wood and use it in the correct way will never change. When I build a shed, the feeling of being linked to thousands of years of ancestors is one that I find humbling and inspiring. It is as though I am showing respect to past generations and in my own way I am helping to celebrate our craft traditions and our creative history.

The significance runs deeper still than respect for our ancestral history, there is something that happens when you spend long periods around wood. The dimensions seem familiar, its soft firmness feels comfortable and comforting. I have thought a lot about this over the years, I often wonder about the effect hundreds of thousands of years of working with wood and the undoubted advantage gained by those who could build well with wood has had on humans. Wooden shelters go right back to the beginnings of human existence and they have played a part in our evolution and at this point the connection goes further than that of the conscious mind and approaches the spiritual.

As I sit here now, in the little writing corner of my shed trying to summarise this book, the overriding feeling I have is that I want other people to be able to experience the simple but pure joy of being in a place like this. It is not a joy filled with excitement or passion, it is a quiet happiness. As I look to my left, towards the angled window which faces south, I can feel the slight warmth of the winter sun on my hands and face. It shines through my uncanvassed picture frames and casts an abstract pattern of squares onto the floor. I can smell a mixture of pine resin, dust and coffee, and I can hear through my medium quality Roberts radio one of the late string quartets of Beethoven and floating around the music are the enchanting sounds of the local song thrush which often joins me at this time of day to celebrate its own successes.

I don't know the best way to describe these experiences, perhaps if I could they wouldn't be so special. I've heard it talked about as mindfulness, but there is also a kind of utilitarian pleasure that is the companion of right thinking, the result of the work I am doing here. If I was forced to distil it to one word, it might be contentment. There is nothing spectacular or extravagant about my shed, but these little moments of peace within it are the ones that I most often remember at the end of a day when the other parts of my life have disappeared into a cacophony of discussions, plans and tasks.

I realise now that not only has my shed become a part of me, I have become a part of my shed. Every time I walk down the garden path I create these moments because I expect them, I become one with my shed and this is the closest description I can get to explaining the art of being shed. I think this is part of the reason I built the shed in the first place, a subconscious calling to make a place that my heart called for.

These experiences are accessible to all. For a relatively small amount of money anyone can build a shed, but this small act is something that can completely change the way you live and the way you understand life. The shed has few boundaries, they exist outside of social or professional class, as I have shown in the case studies, they can be of equal value to music producers, ecologists, carpenters, artists, shipping brokers or journalists. The shed can provide a means to create whatever it is you feel is missing from your life or it can make the pursuit of a dream possible.

I finish how I started with some words from the great shed man himself Henry David Thoreau upon his return from his Walden wilderness:

'I learned this, at least, by my experiment: that if one advances confidently in the direction of his dreams, and endeavours to live the life which he has imagined, he will meet with a success unexpected in common hours.'

After all is said and done, you will never regret building a shed, but you may well regret never doing so. Once you have a shed of your own, you will concern yourself less with the problems that enter your world through the TV screen of your living room. I would urge you to not tolerate the monotony of modern convention because the problem with a smooth and comfortable, event-free life is that it is a smooth and comfortable, event-free life. So, if you don't yet have plans to build a shed, then get busy working on some, become a part of the great ancestral traditions of human build craft. Have faith and a determination to follow your shed dream through to its conclusion and your life will be all the better for it.

USEFUL TERMS

Foundations:	The means by which the structure is connected, and the structure load transferred, to the ground.
Planning Permission:	Permission to build a structure obtained from the Local Council. Not to be confused with Building Regulations.
Building Regulations:	Permission given by the Local Council to build a structure according to official Building Regulations. Most structures over a m² floor area will need to meet these regulations.
Postcrete:	Tradename for pre-mixed, quick-drying cement mix.
Hardcore:	Broken bricks, rubble or similar solid material used as a filling or foundation in a building.
MOT:	Graded crushed stone hardcore used as a pre- or lower base in construction surfaces.
Kingspan:	Tradename for thermal insulation boards.
Celotex:	Tradename for thermal insulation boards.
Plywood:	A type of strong, thin wooden board consisting of two or more layers glued together, with the direction of the grain altering.
OSB:	Oriented Strand Board. Also known as strand board or Sterling Board. Sheet timber manufactured using adhesives and compressing, with strands or flakes of wood. Available in various sizes and thickness.
Plasterboard:	Board made of plaster set between two sheets of paper used especially to form or line the inner walls of a building.

Rockwool:	Trade-name for mineral wool, an inorganic matted fibre used for insulation and soundproofing.
Visqueen:	Tradename for waterproof membrane used under construction concrete.
Noggings:	Short pieces of timber used as braces between framework.
Cladding:	The weather-protecting skin over any construction.
DPM:	Damp-Proof Membrane.
Breathable Membrane:	A water resistant but air permeable material.
Firrings:	Wooden strips cut on an angle to create fall on a flat roof.
Batten:	Long strips of timber used to hold cladding to walls and roofs.
EPDM:	Ethylene Propylene Diene Monomer. Durable synthetic rubber roofing membrane.
Joists:	A length of timber or steel supporting part of the structure of a building.
Rafters:	Sloping timber roof supports.
Trusses:	Pre-formed triangular roof supports.
Purlins:	Horizontal roof timbers used to support rafters or trusses.
Green Oak:	Oak that is newly cut, usually inside the last 6 months.
UPVC:	Unplasticised Polyvinyl Chloride. Chemically resistant form of PVC used for making windows, doors and pipework.

TIMBER JOIST SPAN TABLES

When building timber roofs, ceilings and floors, you will need to work out whether the choice of wood, both in quality and size, is strong enough for its purpose without needing extra support. The following tables can be used to help make those calculations. However, if the build is subject to 'building control' then the building inspector may ask for additional engineer's calculations.

The weight of a timber floor consists of the structural joists, the floorboards and any fixings. This is known as 'the dead load' and the joists must be able to support this dead load without sag. Engineers generally consider this to be a maximum of 0.5 kilonewtons per square metre (KN/m^2). Add to this the weight that will be placed upon the floor, by furniture and general footfall, which is known as 'the imposed load' which is usually accepted for normal use to be a maximum of $1.5KN/m^2$.

The guides below use timber of strength grading C16. To use the tables, you will need to measure the suspended area of the joist, the distance between each joist to the centres and the size of the timber.

The following table is calculated for a dead load of more than $0.25KN/m^2$ but no more than $0.50KN/m^2$ and allows for an imposed load to a maximum of $1.5KN/m^2$.

Recommended Maximum Spans for Floor Joists

Joist Size	400mm	450mm	600mm
Area (mm)	Span (m)	Span (m)	Span (m)
50 x 100	2.08	1.97	1.67
50 x 125	2.66	2.56	2.30
50 x 150	3.27	3.14	2.86
50 x 175	3.77	3.62	3.29

The following tables are a guide only, they are based on a standard UK snowfall allowance of 0.75KN/m² and allowances should be made for ventilation requirements when using insulation as well as green roof manufacturers' guidelines.

Recommended Maximum Spans for Flat and Pitched Roofs

Rafter size	Maximum spans measured between any supports			
C16 Timber	Angle 22.5°–30°		31°–45°	
Spacings	400mm	600mm	400mm	600mm
50 x 100mm	2.45m	2.14m	2.53m	2.21m
50 x 125mm	3.05m	2.67m	3.15m	2.76m
50 x 150mm	3.65m	3.20m	3.76m	3.30m

Flat Roof Joists

Maximum spans measured between any supports

C16 Timber	400mm centres	600mm centres
50 x 125mm	2.53m	2.37m
50 x 150mm	3.19m	2.97m
50 x 175mm	3.81m	3.47m
50 x 200mm	4.48m	3.97m
50 x 225mm	5.09m	4.47m

MY SHED BOOKSHELF

Tiny Homes: Simple Shelter
Lloyd Kahn (Shelter Publications, 2012)

Wood: Identification & Use
Terry Porter (GMC Publications, 2006)

Small Eco Houses: Living Green in Style
Francesc Zamora Mola et al. (Universe, 2010)

George Clarke's More Amazing Spaces
George Clarke and Jane Field-Lewis (Quadrille, 2014)

Walden
Henry David Thoreau (Macmillan Collectors Library, 2016)

My Tiny Veg Plot
Lia Leendertz (Pavilion, 2015)

RHS Botany for Gardeners
Geoff Hodge (Mitchell Beazley, 2013)

Useful Work v. Useless Toil
William Morris (Penguin, 2008)

Death of a Salesman
Arthur Miller (Penguin, 2000)

Collected Poems 1934–53
Dylan Thomas (Phoenix, 2000)

On Being a Sculptor
Henry Moore (Tate, 2010)

Seven Pillars of Wisdom
T. E. Lawrence (Wordsworth Editions, 1997)

Kiss Kiss
Roald Dahl (Penguin, 1975)

Tao Te Ching
Lao Tzu (Kyle Cathie Limited, 1998)

. . .

Gustav Mahler: The Symphonies
Beethoven: The Late Quartets

ACKNOWLEDGEMENTS

Thank you to John Phelan (the human how-to guide), to Robert Ball (my chippie guru) and Nicky Evans (right-hand man).

Thank you to all the participants in the book and to all the shed users across the globe who make the world a better place to be in.

Say hello or tell me your own shed stories @MrJoelBird and visit www.JoelBird.com.